MODERN
LOCKDOWN

To,
Dear Mark
With Best Wishes,

Dr JK Sharma

Praise for the book

The AMTZ has become a flagbearer of the growth of medical technology in India; a country which until recently was import dependent, is now an exporter of RT-PCR and PPE kits, ventilators, oxygen concentrators and many other products. This book is a versatile account of the AMTZ and how an Indian scientist, Dr Jitendra Sharma, led the AMTZ from concept to spectacular success.

—Amitabh Kant
CEO, NITI Aayog

Made in Lockdown is an inspiring read on how India is headed towards achieving a major and important milestone of becoming atmanirbhar Bharat in medical devices, through the AMTZ and Kalam Institute of Health Technology. These institutions are an outcome of patient and steadfast leadership, coupled with pragmatic implementation. The team's relentless efforts towards meeting the increasing demand of medical devices during the pandemic under trying conditions are worth a read.

—Prof. K. VijayRaghavan
Principal scientific advisor to the Government of India

This book is a beautiful commentary on India's trailblazing innings in medical equipment manufacturing, led by Dr Jitendra Sharma. The AMTZ has transformed India from an overdependent importer of medical devices to a global exporter of medical equipment, even under the extremely trying times of the COVID-19 pandemic.

—Virender Sehwag
Former Indian cricketer

MADE IN LOCKDOWN

India's MedTech Growth Powered by AMTZ

JITENDRA SHARMA

RUPA

Published by
Rupa Publications India Pvt. Ltd 2022
7/16, Ansari Road, Daryaganj
New Delhi 110002

Sales Centres:
Allahabad Bengaluru Chennai
Hyderabad Jaipur Kathmandu
Kolkata Mumbai

ISBN: 978-93-5520-306-9

First impression 2022

10 9 8 7 6 5 4 3 2 1

Dedicated to patients, healthcare and life
And to two teachers—Dr M.R. Patel and
Dr A.N. Safaya who taught us
How our work guards these together.

CONTENTS

FOREWORD

I met Dr Jitendra Sharma in 2015. He was representing India's Ministry of Health and Family Welfare (MoHFW) at the World Congress on Medical Physics and Biomedical Engineering organized by the International Federation of Medical and Biological Engineering (IFMBE) in Toronto. I led in partnership with the World Health Organization (WHO). He had this wonderful background and a track record of accomplishment at the National Health Systems Resource Centre (NSHRC). Later that year, we were together in Hangzhou, China for the first International Clinical Engineering and Health Technology Management Congress by the IFMBE and formed a significant bond. But little did I know what was in store for this lovable and driven young man.

Since those initial meetings, we have been personal friends and professional colleagues. I had the privilege of visiting the Andhra Pradesh MedTech Zone (AMTZ) in December 2018 and have had a front-row seat to the incredible story you are about to read. Further, 'the audacity of hope' that Dr Sharma describes connects not only our heads but our hearts as well—it is hope that drives deep action and recognizes the favour of divine intervention.

In May 2020, as COVID-19 had hit the world with fury, the WHO convened its 194 member states for their annual meeting. A key gap expressed by the ministers of health and other government executives was the global need for more life-saving medical devices such as ventilators. The next year, these same leaders called out for more medical oxygen. By 2021, management strategies for traditional medical devices as well as digital health tools, personal protective equipment (PPE) and the full range of oxygen production and treatment systems had become the work of those in the health technology profession, in which Dr Sharma and I serve.

In the 1990s, my colleagues in the United States of America (USA) and I decided to begin training global health leaders in the management of health technologies. The WHO formalized this global need with their 2007 resolution. By 2015, our professional group had conducted this training for 90 countries, including the programme where I met Dr Sharma. The WHO notes that these responsibilities are typically carried out by healthcare team members called clinical (or biomedical) engineers. Dr Sharma came in with a doctorate in healthcare management and already having founded health technology management capability for India's MoHFW. He had also already served as a consultant to the World Bank and the WHO. He had begun to understand how the complex mix of government, market forces, policy, academia and industry could come together powerfully for good.

Rarely before has there been the need to combine various national and global tools to use our profession to help solve a global challenge optimally. An example would be when the US-based health technology leader, Dr Yadin David, was called on to work with Israel's prime minister and the US vice president to offer telemedicine tools to Jordan as a part of the Middle East peace process in the late 1990s. *Made in Lockdown* chronicles another important story of how the rapid rise and development of a new health technology ecosystem allowed an unbelievable national and international response to the global pandemic.

In 2009, there was a change in leadership at the WHO in the health technologies (medical device) area. Adriana Velazquez, a biomedical engineer from Mexico, came into that role of Lead, Medical Devices for the WHO. That same year, our global professional organization, the IFMBE's Clinical Engineering Division (CED), elected Dr David as its chair. Since that time, the WHO and the CED have worked together to improve global health technology management capabilities. I joined the CED Board in 2015 and was elected as chair in 2018. The WHO and the CED added a newly created partner in 2020, called the Global Clinical Engineering Alliance (GCEA). Together, we have been able to provide a network of health technology management leaders in 170 countries and the global research capability allowing us to address COVID-19-sized challenges.

I have known and stayed in communication with Dr Sharma over the years. His courage, energy and vision continue to astonish. For example, in the last six years, he has earned two more doctorates. He was able to make use of this continuing education in several ways—for example, first, to develop academia-industry linkages for India's national innovation policy. Second, to help develop the production linked incentive (PLI) scheme, one of three major policy tools he has facilitated with the government to allow their 'medical devices made in India' plans to succeed.

So, the AMTZ's activities bringing hundreds of Indian manufacturers together all in one place to maximize collaboration, innovation and production through 18 shared scientific centres during COVID-19 has led to startling results. This has been accomplished both according to the needs of India and through open hands to help others with huge daily production of critical medical devices, laboratory tests, PPE, digital tools and more.

Dr Sharma does all this with great humility and the wonderful dedication of his team, consisting of individuals from eminent institutions of science globally. His stated goal is to 'democratize medical technologies', so that all countries can have access to the fruits of the AMTZ's and India's labour. A current example is the just-operationalized centre for manufacturing and supply of artificial arms, limbs, myoelectric and bionic organs at the AMTZ offering many low-cost novel assistive technologies. Another is Dr Sharma's proposal shared recently with health technology colleagues from 128 countries on development of medical devices design capabilities sharable on open-source platforms. He further proposed that for medical device projects that require high-investment capabilities, with affordability in mind, consortiums from academia and industry could be established for collaboration with the global health technology stakeholders.

I am privileged to know Dr Sharma very well. We both have been given and share platforms to take action. This is characterized in his book as: 'Hope in the face of difficulty. Hope in the face of uncertainty. The audacity of hope.' But also, hope grounded in the certainty of divine intervention. This intervention was demonstrated in several ways in 2018 when the AMTZ was being built. One example was, the construction of the AMTZ Convention Centre within 78 days, well in time to host the December 2020 WHO Global Forum. Or specifically, at a very critical time when the Creator withheld rain so that a massive concrete roof could be laid without delay or damage. I wish readers a rejuvenating experience while reading all the stories in this great book and again, be amazed!

Tom Judd
Chairman, Clinical Engineering Division, IFMBE
21 November 2021

INTRODUCTION

Every crisis is an opportunity for nation-building. When the world went into lockdown due to the unprecedented, global COVID crisis, the same proved true for the newly visualized, Andhra Pradesh MedTech Zone (AMTZ), Asia's first, exclusive medical devices technology and manufacturing zone. It is now one of the world's largest medical equipment manufacturing and development cluster, set up to overcome India's huge import dependency on medical devices. The AMTZ, silently, went full steam ahead to beat the biggest public healthcare crisis of our times, by undertaking the design and manufacturing of critical COVID-19 related medical devices at an unprecedented speed. This went a long way in supporting our collective drive to beat COVID-19.

In the process, the AMTZ has lit the fire of the MedTech revolution in the country and has set India firmly on the course to become a self-reliant innovation hub for medical devices. Since 2018–19, i.e., exactly when the AMTZ came into existence, the import of medical devices saw a contraction, for the first time in history. India's expanding domestic market and its expanding exports are also staying firmly on course. At this rate, with the AMTZ leading the way, India may achieve complete import neutrality by 2024–25.

This is the story of a unique national vision; the power of a dream, of leadership, motivation and achieving impossible tasks and targets against numerous odds— because the healthcare sovereignty of the country is non-negotiable and paramount. This is a story akin to the Green Revolution or the White Revolution. Each of them made India a global powerhouse in a specific sector, and that is exactly what the AMTZ is doing in the critical medical device sector to make healthcare a near reality instead of a distant dream.

Self-reliance in the development and manufacturing of medical devices is a critical component of national healthcare and national security as well. The AMTZ, with its record-making milestones, is helping the country make a firm and swift transition from import dependency to becoming a global innovation hub and, desirably, a net exporter.

This book is a fascinating and inspiring account of how a newly visualized institution, rose to the occasion and with an untiring spirit, led medical technology to the forefront of attention.

This is also a first-of-its-kind book about this lesser-understood subject of medical technology to be published in India, even though medical devices are as much an integral part of our day-to-day life as medicine or food.

This book has been purposely written in a manner that can be enjoyed and appreciated by the medical fraternity, researchers, industry professionals as well as common readers while providing deep insights and experiences of many a milestone.

I hope you will enjoy reading this book.

1

AMAR AKBAR ANTHONY AND BEYOND...

I f you are reading this book using a pair of spectacles, you are already a user of medical devices. Contrary to the perception that only something as gigantic as a magnetic resonance imaging (MRI) machine could be a medical device, our lives are surrounded by products that make our lives safer and improve its quality. Whether it's a thermometer at home, stethoscope in clinics, an ambulance to reach a health facility or cardiac or respiratory care monitors in hospitals, each of these life-saving or life-benefiting products has been created by a relatively unknown 'subspecies' of humans known as biomedical engineers. From the self-test pregnancy kit that can be used in the comfort of one's own home to a treadmill in a gym; a Fit-bit smartwatch on our wrist or a pacemaker that helps regulate heartbeat; most of us do not realize how medical devices impact and sustain our day-to-day life and lives at large. Besides, we have a vast spectrum of an unaccounted ever-growing list—from N95 masks to X-ray and COVID-19 reverse transcription-polymerase chain reaction (RT-PCR) kit to an MRI; the expanse is huge. And unlike pharmaceutical products, it is uncannily diverse. Even in the Bollywood movie *Amar Akbar Anthony*, hilarious cinematic liberty resulted in the three protagonists, unbeknownst to the fact that they are brothers, deciding to donate blood to save an elderly lady who happens to be their mother! Yes, even the blood cross-matching kit used to categorize blood into groups, is a medical device. Medical devices, therefore, form the backbone of healthcare, their more well-known siblings being pharmaceutical drugs and vaccines. Here is a short introduction to pillars that make modern healthcare:

(i) **First pillar:** The policy of health is the eldest of the family. This includes principles such as insurance, coverage limits, costs for reimbursement, complementarity of public and private sector services, medical education and everything that allows or inhibits people from accessing healthcare.

(ii) **Second pillar:** Healthcare professionals signifying the intellectual and service workforce consisting of our doctors, paramedics, technicians and other support staff and all those engaged in service delivery.

(iii) **Third pillar:** The physical infrastructure of hospitals, the building including the safety systems, the oxygen pipelines, the electrical, water and fire safety infrastructure and every other aspect of a hospital.

(iv) **Fourth pillar:** Medicines, vaccines and blood products—therapeutic elements of care which treats or heals due to pharmacological or physiological action. These are also the most common products that the public is aware of, and is constantly dealing with, from pharmacy shops to blood banks.

(v) **Fifth pillar:** Medical technology is the most diverse, complex and heterogeneous group of products, and is generally used or purchased by care providers and hospitals. Their application requires specialized training and not just consumption, as may be in the case of pharmaceutical drugs. Tools and technologies that are diagnostics, curative, operative, rehabilitative and preventive and the machines that allow restoration to a comprehensive state of health. These technologies are extremely complex and dependent on associated systems such as oxygen, electricity, highly purified environments such as clean rooms, operation theatres or intensive care units (ICUs).

For a robust, sustainable and inclusive healthcare ecosystem, all five pillars must be equally evolved and harmonized in developing nations including India. Affordable healthcare is a critical necessity for the healthcare security of the nation as much as a reason for the health, happiness and economic productivity of families, directly impacting societal progress.

Without healthcare security—which includes an affordable, accessible and quality healthcare edifice, largely reliant on home-grown resources—a country of the size and with complexities like India would forever run the risk of being dependent on costly and preventable imports. It could raise the cost of healthcare. Expensive healthcare, in turn, entails the risk of deprivation of universal and quality healthcare to a large section of society, leading to further societal implications and divide. Above all, it could seriously deprive or limit the country of demographic dividends.

The recorded history of medical devices that goes as far back as 3000 BCE is also nearly as old as that of medicine. Egyptians were known to have used surgical instruments. The first treatise on surgery was written way back in 2700 BCE by Imhotep, who served as the vizier of Pharaoh Djoser and was a renowned physician and surgeon, so much so that he was later deified as a god of medicine by Egyptians. The Edwin Smith Papyrus, dating 1600 BCE, is a manual describing the procedure of performing traumatic surgery and gives 48 case histories. Evidence of surgery, implying the use of medical devices, is even older in India, dating back to the Indus Valley civilization and pre-Harappan days. Research on skulls from those ruins has revealed that teeth drilling was practised in these areas as far back as 7000 BCE!

Rishi Sushruta, known as the 'founding father of surgery in India' and considered to have lived between 1200 and 600 BCE, much before Rishi Charaka (100–

200 BCE, the author of the famed *Charak Samhita*, a grand medical treatise), in his book *Sushruta Samhita* describes in detail, amongst other things, procedures on performing various forms of cosmetic surgery plastic surgery, and even rhinoplasty. Sushruta describes 120 surgical instruments, 300 surgical procedures and classification of human surgeries in eight categories.

Path-breaking innovations in medical devices and medical technology began in the mid-nineteenth century and gathered momentum at the beginning of the twentieth century. But many of the things that we take for granted were invented as early as the fourteenth century or even before that. For example, the ubiquitous reading glasses of today were invented around the thirteenth century and it is widely accepted that Italians were the first ones to use them. The first thermometers were called thermoscopes, and the Italian inventor Santorio Santorio was the first to put a numerical scale on the temperature measuring instrument.[1] Daniel Gabriel Fahrenheit (1686–1736), the German physicist who had earlier invented the alcohol thermometer in 1709, invented the first mercury thermometer, the prototype for what came to be known

---

[1] G. Eknoyan, 'Santorio Sanctorius (1561–1636)—Founding Father of Metabolic Balance Studies', *American Journal of Nephrology*, Vol. 19, 1999, pp 226–233. Accessed on 23 December 2021.

as the modern thermometer in 1714. At the start of the seventeenth century, there was no way to quantify heat. In 1724, Fahrenheit introduced the temperature scale that bears his name: the Fahrenheit scale. The Celsius scale was invented by Swedish astronomer Anders Celsius (1701–1744) around the same time. However, the use of medical instruments in diagnosis made its dramatic mark much later, with the invention of the stethoscope in the early nineteenth century. The first stethoscope, invented in 1816 by the French physician, Dr René-Théophile-Hyacinthe Laennec (1781–1826), was made of wood. It was a kind of wooden pipe inspired by the flute. This simple invention has had a profound impact on medical diagnosis and remains the most utilized and recognizable symbol of a medical practitioner to date.

Laennec's first seminal work on the use of listening to body sounds, *De L'auscultation Mediate* (On Mediate Auscultation) and his first descriptions of bronchiectasis, cirrhosis and classification of pulmonary conditions such as pneumonia, pneumothorax and other lung diseases based on the sounds he had heard with his invention, formed the first set of practical applications using the stethoscope.

The next big development was the invention of hypodermic (relating to the region immediately beneath the skin) syringes, independently and around the same time in 1853, by Charles Gabriel Pravaz (1791–1853) and Alexander Wood (1817–1884). Today, one can't imagine medical treatment without these syringes, and despite many improvisations, the basic functioning principle and design remain the same.

Ophthalmoscope, an instrument used for examining the interior structures of the eye, especially the retina, was also designed around the mid-nineteenth century by Hermann von Helmholtz (1821–1894). Helmholtz is considered one of the first biomedical engineers. Though others had independently created such a device before, it was not until Helmholtz's invention that the usefulness of the device became widely recognized.

The next modern MedTech was the discovery of the X-ray by Wilhelm Roentgen (1845–1923), a physicist and mechanical engineer. Roentgen produced and detected X-rays or Rontgen rays on 8 November 1895, an achievement that earned him the first Nobel Prize in Physics in 1901. Roentgen being a great humanist donated the entire reward from his Nobel Prize to research at his university, the University of Wurzburg. And like Pierre Curie, Roentgen deeply wished society to benefit from his discovery and refused to take patents related to his discovery of X-rays. Till date, X-rays remain a core principle applied in clinical diagnosis, particularly in pulmonary and orthopaedic specialties. Subsequently, the first practical electrocardiogram (ECG or EKG) was invented in 1895 by Willem Einthoven (1860–1927), who eventually received the Nobel Prize in Medicine in 1924 for this invention. The invention completely enhanced diagnostic capabilities and let to establishment of cardiology, which until then, being a matter of the 'heart', was considered too complex.

The twentieth century galvanized modern medicine with evolving medical technology, even further. In 1923, Eliot Cutler performed the world's first successful heart valve surgery whereas in 1925, Marius Smith-Petersen invented the nail implant to secure the bone in hip fractures. Within two years, in 1927, Philip Drinker invented an iron lung, also known as a tank ventilator or Drinker tank, and is a type of negative pressure ventilator (NPV). First paper on Diagnostic Ultrasound was published in 1942 by Dr Karl Theodore Dussik leading to the development of ultrasonography technology. Artificial Kidney by Carl Walter, John Merrill and George Thorn in 1947, Mitral valve in 1948, first cardiac pacemaker in 1950 by John Hopps lifted the practice of medicine into realms of implants and organ support.

In the second half of the twentieth century, discoveries and application of science to evolve medical technologies continued at a rapid pace. While the technique of long-term storage of human blood was perfected by 1964, the first human heart transplant was performed by Dr Christian Bernard which became a landmark in the history of modern surgery. In 1968, as Mass General Hospital demonstrated telemedicine, technology further started to influence medical practices. Development of the intra-aortic balloon catheter in 1969 at MIT, development of positron emission tomography (PET) scan and that of magnetic resonance imaging, by the end of the '80s, most of them led by MIT, positioned America as a hub of modern MedTech research.

Some great innovations were taking place elsewhere too. By 1985, the genetic fingerprinting method had been devised; and the artificial kidney dialysis machine had been developed.

While 1900–1950 saw tremendous growth and development of medical technology in the western world, in the Indian subcontinent, under British rule, a few small pockets where surgical instruments were manufactured, emerged and flourished over time. These budding centres also made their mark in Europe and in the US. The most notable example was the city of Sialkot in erstwhile Punjab, which was part of pre-Partition India. Sialkot became a hub for the production of steel precision surgical tools, thanks, largely, to the natural skills of the metal artisans of this region and the encouragement provided by the British and American Missionaries, who ran a hospital in town. They were impressed with the skills of the local blacksmiths who replicated imported instruments with great finesse. They encouraged local businessmen to set up manufacturing units of surgical instruments. Exports of surgical instruments to the US and Europe started in the early 1930s given the lesser cost and comparable quality of these instruments that were made in Sialkot. To institutionalize the local expertise of manufacturing surgical instruments and provide common facilities to the manufacturers, the British government established the Metal Industries Development Centre (MIDC) in Sialkot in 1941. This move helped the industry progress from manufacturing basic surgical tools to precision surgical instruments.

After Independence in 1947, the health sector, as a whole, and medical technology in particular, grew only at a moderate pace in India. The budgetary resource allocation for the health sector remained limited to approximately 1 per cent of the gross domestic product (GDP) as against the 8–12 per cent of the GDP in advanced nations, leading to lesser penetration of advance techniques or more widespread use of medical technology.[2] And despite a booming pharmaceutical industry, serving nearly the entire globe with affordable medicines, India has remained import dependent to the extent of over 80 per cent in medical devices with over 95 per cent in advanced technological segments such as MRIs or CT scanners.[3] An unbelievable anomaly came to exist, where a country could send a space probe to Mars but could not yet make a PET-CT scan system for cancer diagnosis. Medical devices continued to remain the weakest link in the pursuit of India's health goals and a limitation in our healthcare value chain. More recent episodes of shortage of oxygen concentrators in the second wave of the COVID-19 pandemic only repositioned this argument, even stronger.

This situation would have been of lesser disadvantage in the '70s and '80s. The modern inventions and innovations in medical devices/medical technologies, which would fundamentally alter and elevate medical practices around the world to a hitherto-unimaginable level, had not yet become popular nor had they become a

---

[2] 'GLOBEXIM 2020–21', Kalam Institute of Health Technology, 2020.
[3] Ibid.

critical mass of diagnostics and curative instrumentation. Until the '80s, pharmaceuticals played a bigger and more decisive role in healthcare compared to medical technologies and also had a bigger share in the overall healthcare cost basket. As pointed out earlier, while 1900–1950 saw the emergence of several path-breaking technologies, from the 1970s, new innovations in medical technologies were going to have a more profound impact on medical practice and would have a far greater bearing on the healthcare sector globally.

Given that building the medical technology sector requires deeper investments in research, longer incubation periods and structured educational programmes around biomedical engineering, it would not be an exaggeration to say that the medical device sector remained the neglected orphan sector of the Indian healthcare ecosystem over the decades. This had a serious impact on healthcare expenditure and above all, on the healthcare security of the nation. Overdependence on the import of medical devices, expanding healthcare coverage and improvement in paying capacity for better medical care, eventually made India a country with over 80 per cent dependence on imports of medical devices, with an import bill of about ₹50,000 crore per annum just on medical devices.

The Rising Significance of Medical Technologies: The Kalam-Raju Stent Era

The 1991 liberalization set the stage for dramatic changes encompassing all spheres of economic activities. The liberalization also resulted in a sharp rise in household income, which, coupled with some amazing advances in medical technology and the introduction of new-age smart medical devices, had a profound impact on the growth and consumption pattern of medical devices. From 1991 to around 2005, the market for medical devices expanded phenomenally but continued to be largely served through imports. And the primary consumers remained medical practitioners and hospitals.

The 1990s brought forth advancements in medical technologies that caught the world's imagination. The use of silicon chips in electronic equipment became popular and made medical equipment smaller and cheaper. The elite club—the US, Germany, Japan, to name a few—made stoic advancements in research on MedTech and rapidly patented some of the latest findings on the path of discovery. Furthermore, the internet rapidly bridged the information gap between health practitioners, technology applications and the adoption of modern devices. Medical technology started to flow from the western world to emerging economies like India in an unprecedented manner. This started to have several implications on medical practices, healthcare cost and development of a new niche industry. The biggest impact on modern medical devices from a clinical perspective was on diagnostics and surgeries. Surgery, which till about the '70s was still considered an offshoot of a 'barbaric' process, transformed itself with advancements in anaesthesia technologies, ICU care products and laparoscopy. Drastic advances came in radiology imaging putting the MRIs and CT scanners in the market, well within the reach of affluent although not within the resources of common folks.

The advancement in medical technologies also gave rise to new niche and sophisticated products such as the biosensors, components, medical electronics and biomaterials. In addition to the development of this new industry, factors such as income jumps, ease of availability of packaged foods, urbanization and sedentary lifestyle resulted in a quantum jump of new-age diseases or lifestyle diseases such as obesity-induced diabetes, heart disease, hypertension, etc. Most of them required lifelong care and dependency on medical products, including self-health and home health monitoring devices. Then came the internet of things (IoT) and Bluetooth, which allowed a bunch of 'smart' consumer goods to be integrated. While a simple thermometer became a standard fixture in an average household, people started keeping relatively sophisticated devices such as glucometer (sugar testing device) and, now, smart watches, to stay healthy and fit. The jump in consumption of medical technologies in hospitals and common households did not, however, synchronize with the jump in production capacity and access to know-how.

Therefore, while a new expenditure category got added to the healthcare basket, more and more dependence on import became an unavoidable reality. Although, the size and growth of the medical device market was not well-documented before 2010, the data available for subsequent years gives us a fair insight into how prominently it grew and become a big part of healthcare vis–à–vis medicines.

As of 2020, India produces about $40 billion worth of pharma products, half of which is exported. India is now the largest producer of generic medicines by volume and has rightly earned the epithet of 'the pharmacy capital of the world'. India can meet over 90 per cent of its pharmaceutical requirement with domestic production.[4]

---

[4]Ibid.

The net balance of trade is heavily tilted in favour of India and remained a cause of lesser worry, except for the import of some critical active pharmaceutical ingredients (APIs) and the lack of novel molecules—two aspects that posed some challenge to Indian pharma.

On the other hand, the market size of the medical devices industry in India is estimated to be around $8 billion, with imports exceeding $6 billion. Such high dependency and import costs posed a really daunting situation, given the high number of patents and intellectual property rights associated with each medical device, the value chain of components, know-how and requirement of installation and training. If there is to be a solution to this situation, it has to be comprehensive and not just production.[5]

From a fraction of the cost factor prior to 1990s, when medical devices generally constituted simple surgical items, syringes, stethoscope and the likes, MedTech and innovations became a key factor driving up healthcare costs. The Kalam-Raju stent and successes of this nature were a few milestones that sufficiently proved the capability of minds in the Indian medical devices landscape. But the capacity to run a hospital,

---

[5]Ibid.

largely with Indian-made medical devices, remained a very distant hope. To some extent, an ecosystem was missing which could convert capability into capacity. The Kalam-Raju stent was a classic example of how scientific leaders like Dr A.P.J. Abdul Kalam could lead path-breaking work. No wonder, cardiac stents are one of the device segments, wherein India does not depend largely on imports with over 10 cardiac stents makers spread across the country—SMT, Translumia, Meril, to name a few, competing successfully with their foreign cousins such as Boston Scientific, Johnson & Johnson and St Jude. The irony is that the success story of the cardiac stent did not get replicated into other medical device segments.

In the absence of a nurturing environment, despite the presence of a huge market, engineering capabilities, and capital resources, we were not able to develop many home-grown billion-dollar medical device companies. In fact, the lack of a supportive ecosystem led to many home-grown medical device manufacturing companies closing down, allowing only a few courageous and competitive ones to survive.

The 'Make in India' initiative suddenly recognized the importance of value chain manufacturing and medical device subsequently became a flagship sector. However, it took a calamity as big as the COVID-19 crisis—when even RT-PCR and PPE became household names—for the real potential and opportunity in this sector to be recognized.

As medical devices deal with life-saving functions of the human body, the development and manufacturing of medical devices call for extra care and deeper knowledge and come loaded with a myriad of regulations. And then, there are added complexities of intellectual property rights (IPR) issues and process know-how.

Developing the medical device sector requires policy support, financial assistance and the development of a knowledge bank whereby research and innovations could be shared easily with the industry. No piecemeal and disjointed solution could work. The development of a robust, home-grown medical device sector requires an integrated, amalgamative and innovative approach— the creation of a nest or a few nests which could truly nurture the development of products, provide a base for rigorous product testing in complex laboratories, a catalytic hub which could play the part of friend and guide to manufacturers, industry and entrepreneurs.

It was this requirement that led to the idea of setting up India's first and perhaps the world's only medical equipment manufacturing park, now popularly called the

AMTZ—the A to Z of medical devices. Over a short span of three years, the AMTZ, along with support institutions such as the Kalam Institute of Health Technology (KIHT), has become an institution that inspires national pride and functions as a fulcrum of medical device production, thus rocketing India into an increasingly strong position.

The AMTZ and its associated institutions like KIHT were envisioned to play a transformative and catalytic role. The AMTZ ecosystem became a unique global institution where research, innovation, brainstorming, intellectual exchanges and the development and manufacturing of niche medical devices started to take place. As a captain of MedTech infrastructure and fountainhead of MedTech research, it married two unusual approaches—the mix of models from Homi J. Bhabha's Tata Institute of Fundamental Research (TIFR), where science was central to all effort, and Dr Verghese Kurien's Amul—where collaborative production capacities were the focus, into one singular integrated strategy.

But it is easier said than done! A mission to create something as humongous and as complex as a medical equipment manufacturing and research hub had no precedent or examples to follow. The AMTZ story and the manner in which thousands of life-saving products were invented, innovated and produced is both a story of grit as well as strategic deployment of science. In this book, we take you through the tribulations and triumphs of this journey. When the world was in lockdown, there was an ecosystem that operated 24 hours a day, with thousands of men and women silently producing life-saving products. Yes, this is a story of a MedTech city made in lockdown!

2

HELLO 108! BYE-BYE POLIO

Post Independence, India became a member state of the WHO in January 1948, and just 10 months later in October 1948, it earned the distinction as venue for the first session of the WHO Regional Committee for Southeast Asia.

The Declaration of Alma-Ata in September 1978 called on all the member states of the United Nations (UN) to formulate a national health policy with a major thrust on primary healthcare. It established health as a fundamental human right and ushered in an accountable and responsible concept of public healthcare.

After over 35 years of becoming a member of the WHO, India witnessed the introduction of the first-ever National Health Policy in 1983 with an emphatic call for universal healthcare i.e., 'Health for All by the year 2000 AD'.[6] In this declaration, 'accessibility and technology' were central to universal healthcare, which went unnoticed for decades.

After the first health policy in 1983, India had to wait for almost two decades for the second health policy to be introduced in 2002 and for another 15 years for the third one in 2017.

A long delay in the policy announcement leads to incoherent policies, fragmented deliverables and a more inefficient healthcare ecosystem in the absence of instructional and directional clarity.

These staggered policies have also taken their toll on indigenization, development, affordability and accessibility to MedTech, particularly as the MedTech demand generation lies in the evolution of the health system itself.

Though there has been a constant demand over the

---

[6]International Conference on Primary Health Care, 'Declaration of Alma-Ata', *WHO Chronicle*, Vol. 32, no. 11, 1978, pp. 428–30.

last two decades for the right to health, which is yet to be acceded to, universal healthcare coverage endeavours have been strengthened to ensure incremental medical care of citizens. Ayushman Bharat is the latest addition to such an endeavour which allowed both private and public sector to participate in healthcare delivery and created a considerable market size for the devices.

Another factor that gave impetus to the development of new-age medical devices or personal care devices was the sharp rise in lifestyle diseases like diabetes, heart conditions, obesity, etc. These diseases require more round-the-clock monitoring as well as greater personal care. This led to the migration of medical devices from hospitals into our homes. Medical devices moved from being just in the diagnostic and surgical arena of hospitals to the domain of personal healthcare.

From the perspective of supply, entrepreneurs and companies were quick to recognize and seize new opportunities. While older, conventional MedTech leaders such as Abbott, Bayer, General Electric Healthcare, Roche, Johnson & Johnson, Medtronic, Philips Healthcare, 3M Healthcare and Indian MedTech companies like BPL Medical Technologies led by Sunil Khurana, Phoenix Medical Systems led by V. Sashi Kumar, Hindustan Syringes and Medical

Devices led by Rajiv Nath, Transasia Biomedicals led by Suresh and Mala Vazirani, Trivitron Healthcare led by Dr G.S.K. Velu and few other home-grown leaders tried to passionately broaden their portfolio and establish specialized divisions for their in-house product development.

But the first large impetus came from the National Health Mission launched in 2005. It was for the first time that India launched three major MedTech based initiatives: the 108 National Ambulance Services with complete medical technology mobile infrastructure, the neo-natal care ICUs; and evolving secondary care infrastructure with emphasis on strengthening district hospitals. With 108 ambulance services encompassing over 22,000 ambulances equipped with life-saving devices, our country welcomed 108 with a 'hello' and soon afterwards breathed a sigh of relief when it bid goodbye to polio, a disease which had crippled the society for several generations. Introduction of a structured ambulance service pan-India and eradication of polio are two comprehensive societal achievements and fundamental shifts that National Health Mission must be credited in its first 10 years (2005–2015) besides several other developments and improvements in health indicators.

As the National Health Mission evolved, by 2016, it had several technology-driven programmes, the programme designs of many of which were led by the author of this book during his tenure with the National Health Systems Resource Centre (NSHRC) under the MoHFW, Government of India (GoI). The National Diagnostics Programme for Pathology, National Teleradiology Programme, National Mobile Medical Unit Programme, to name a few, were quickly and progressively implemented across most of the states in India.

The National Dialysis Programme was announced as a public-private partnership (PPP) on 1 February 2014, as part of the Union Budget. This visionary health programme became an excellent example of how expensive medical technologies can be democratized through progressive and effective converge of the private sector, not just in the supply of dialysis machines but also in the provision of dialysis services. The highlight of the programme was the immense reduction in capital cost to the government. State-of-the-art dialysis centres in every district became a possibility.

How desperately India needed a kidney care programme can be gauged from the fact that every year about 2.2 lakh new patients are diagnosed with end-stage renal disease in India. It results in an additional demand for ₹3.4 crore dialysis sessions. But till the launch of the National Dialysis Programme, the dialysis centres in India, even at the full capacity, could cater to less than half the number of patients that required treatment.[7] Besides, a more prohibiting factor was the cost of dialysis, which reduced drastically as private dialysis service providers competed on the basis of cost per dialysis session, billed to the government, and quoted as low as ₹1,000–1,200 in tenders. At private hospitals outside this programme, the same service cost about ₹4,000 per session.

As part of the service package, service providers started to provide nephrologists, consultants, medical officers, technicians and nurses, reverse osmosis (RO) plants required for the procedure, dialyzers, consumables and, most importantly, the dialysis machine. Since India did not have any local manufacturers for dialysis machines and just one maker of dialyzers in the country, that largely met export requirements, the Indian dialysis market suddenly became investment-worthy.

The proliferation of private pathology laboratories is another good example of the democratization of

[7]'Budget 2016-2017, Speech of Arun Jaitley Minister of Finance', Union Budget: Ministry of Finance, 29 February 2016, indiabudget. gov.in/doc/bspeech/bs201617.pdf. Accessed on 23 December 2021.

medical technology as almost 70 per cent of treatment today requires pathology tests. This has enabled better diagnostic practices and has also brought down the cost of testing. More importantly, the addition of pathology and teleradiology services as part of PPP based programmes under the National Health Mission in 2015, propelled diagnostic test kits manufacturing capabilities. Additionally, many radiology equipment providers such as Allengers, Scanray, Trivitron, to name a few, began to make their mark in the industry. This was modern radiology interfacing with hospital information system (HIS), supported with internet and image transmission. In the pre-IT era, the role of the Indian Space Research Organisation (ISRO) needs to be specially mentioned for the boost it provided to the growth of telemedicine in India. But now, software companies, medical equipment manufacturers and clinicians had a larger and integrated role to play.

While teleradiology was publicly demonstrated by Siemens at the Annual Congress of the Indian Radiology and Imaging Association (IRIA) in 1997, it was only in the early 2000s that teleradiology became popular. The first teleradiology service provider companies in India were Mahajan Imaging, led by the visionary Dr Harsh Mahajan in New Delhi, and later, TeleRad Solutions, led by medical entrepreneur, Dr Arjun Kalyanpur. Teleradiology services started to make a mark in India even for off-shore markets. More teleradiology meant—more of X-ray scanners, digital radiography (DR) systems, picture archiving and communications system (PACS) compatible X-ray machines, MRIs and CT scanners.

My stints as hospital administrator with Sri Satya Sai General Hospital, Puttaparthy and the All India Institute of Medical Sciences (AIIMS), New Delhi, gave me rich insights into two diverse sets of healthcare economics and dynamics. I was fortunate to have the 'father of hospital administration' Dr A.N. Safaya, then director of Sri Satya Sai Hospitals, teaching me the nuances of patient care. At AIIMS, I had the good fortune to train under the supervision of the 'grandmaster' of healthcare, Dr Shakti Gupta, then head of hospital administration and a walking knowledge bank on medical administration. While the former institution offered compassionate health delivery free of cost, the latter was more a national model for low-cost, high-quality tertiary care. But both models had great patient-centricity. The mode of resource mobilization was, again, different at these great institutions. While the former relied on donations to procure high-quality medical equipment, the latter, being an apex public-funded hospital, had the benefit of generous government support. But the common denominator in both the places was the provision of ultra-modern care supported by the rapid adoption of medical technology. Later, when I conceptualized and set up the Health Technology Department at the NSHRC at the MoHFW, while I had the wonderful opportunity to create more and more technology-based programmes, it only meant more and more dependence on imports. It was then that I decided to map the stumbling blocks or entry barriers for indigenous medical device manufacturing. To begin with, I found the absence of testing infrastructure, prototyping facilities, supply chain solution specific to medical devices and, most importantly, an incomplete and unmapped value chain consisting of components across the various segments of medical devices and, in particular, in medical electronics. I had already documented many of the global best practices as a contributor to the WHO report on local production of medical devices in 2011.[8]

Sometime in November 2015, I had requested the forum coordinator of the Association of Indian

---

[8]"Local Production and Technology Transfer to Increase Access to Medical Devices: Addressing the Barriers and Challenges in Low- and Middle-Income Countries', World Health Organization, 2012, https://www.who.int/medical_devices/1240EHT_final.pdf. Accessed on 23 December 2021.

Medical Device Manufacturers (AIMED) to drop by at my office at the NHSRC. As he managed to wind up his work for the day and meet with me by 6.00 p.m., I presented my vision to him. I explained that we lacked an institution where research and development (R&D), testing and validation, component production and manufacturing—all happened in a single ecosystem or cluster. There very thought of setting up a cluster like this was audacious and there did not exist a precedent—not just in medical technology, but in any sector driven by technology. Being a straightforward and frank person, he thoughtfully said, 'This would work wonders! Perhaps in action it would be able to prove that industry does not need the charity of incentives, but a platform of infrastructure to deliver, particularly in high technology complexity segments'. He was a good sounding board, as he could echo the thought process of a much larger group of manufacturers and entrepreneurs, whom he represented. With industry commitment to the cause and no example to emulate, I firmed on my vision and we set off to make further plans to create what would become the MedTech capital of India!

3

A GLANCE AT
THE CHESSBOARD

India's medical device market comprises imports, exports and domestic manufacturing by local and multinational corporations. The import market is valued at ₹44,580.8 crore ($5.9 billion) in the financial year (FY) 2020–21, whereas the exports market reached ₹19,471.2 crore ($2.6 billion).[9] This year, India has had an extra share of PPE kits in its exports due to the COVID-19 pandemic. During the year, India has risen

---

[9]"GLOBEXIM 2020–21', Kalam Institute of Health Technology, 2020.

as a leading manufacturer of PPE kits, which helped the country position itself in the world market to cater to the demand for the kits. We also exported indigenously made COVID-19 testing kits (IgG and RT-PCR kits) to the world. India pivoted the development of these kits through its local knowledge centres and manufacturers and cemented its place as one of the world's top three nations that developed and produced COVID-19 testing kits. Due to restrictions, the quantum of kits exported was low against the demand. Similarly, India positioned itself as the world's second-largest producer of medical textiles.

In 2020–21, India's exports of medical devices grew at 7.0 per cent, whereas imports registered a growth of 7.2 per cent.[10] The growth in imports is attributed to the unabated increase in the number of commodities related to fighting COVID-19 infections. India has witnessed a sharp growth in the import of ventilators, oxygen concentrators, infrared thermometers, COVID-19 testing kits, other in vitro diagnostic (IVD) test kits for post-COVID management (such as D-Dimer, etc.), MRI machines, CT scanners, molecular diagnostic products and in vitro diagnostics analysers. The overall imports and exports of medical devices for the last five financial years are given in the following figures:

---

[10]Ibid.

TABLE 1

Indian Medical Device EXIM Market 2020–21

Medical Device Market	2016–17 (₹ crore)	2017–18 (₹ crore)	2018–19 (₹ crore)	2019–20 (₹ crore)	2020–21 (₹ crore)	YoY (2020–21)	CAGR (per cent)
Indian Medical Device Import Market	30,804.4	35,016.2	43,365.9	41,600.8	44,580.8	7.2 per cent	7.7 per cent
Indian Medical Device Export Market	12,378.1	13,035.0	16,300.0	18,204.3	19,471.2	7.0 per cent	9.5 per cent
Total	43,182.5	48,051.2	59,665.9	59,805.1	64,052.0	7.1 per cent	8.2 per cent

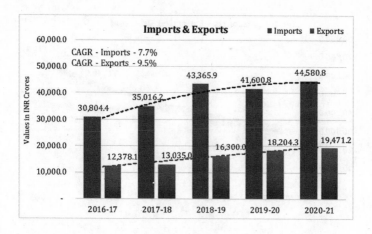

Figure 3.1

India Medical Devices Imports (2016–17 to 2020–21)[11]

Historically, the imports of medical devices were growing at a steep pace, and if the growth rate of imports would have continued as per projections, by 2021, it would have been nearly ₹66,000 crore. The emergence of many interventions has averted the import growth rate, and the actual imports registered a figure of ₹44,580.8 crore, which is 32 per cent lesser than expected. The shrink in imports has been attributed to planned government initiatives to boost local manufacturing and increase the contribution of local manufacturing in the expanding medical device market.

---

[11]Ibid.

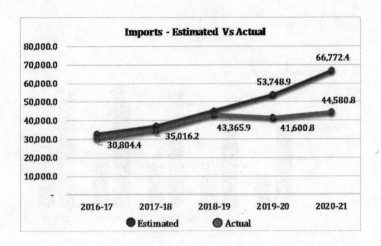

Figure 3.2
Imports—Estimated vs Actual[12]

India has the capital: a scientific pool, a huge resource of biomedical engineers and a new-found zeal for innovation that can offset the burden of legacy. We are certainly well-positioned to change the horoscope of the domestic medical device sector. But for that to happen, there are certain measures we will have to take, both at the policy level and at the level of creation of an integrated and supportive MedTech ecosystem. In turn, it will facilitate competitive manufacturing and promote innovation. Nonetheless, we need to understand that

---

[12]Ibid.

imports also serve certain purposes. Imports can be in the form of technology, skills, machinery, raw materials, joint ventures, capital or outright product import. At the same time, we need to ensure that duties on raw material or inputs resources are low enough to make manufacturing viable and balanced enough not to prohibit the component supply chain from remaining perennially import-dependent. The three strategic policy initiatives given below have tremendous potential to play:

Three Ps that can lead to progress and economic sustainability:

I.   Production-linked incentive (PLI)
II. Phased manufacturing programme (PMP)
III. Public procurement order (PPO)

i. Production-linked incentive (PLI): One of the factors that make medical device manufacturing in India commercially uncompetitive is comparative low-cost imports from other countries. Some countries offer various kinds of tax rebates or cash incentives to boost exports that in turn amount to certain percentage of comparative cost disability in domestically produced medical devices.

So, a device may cost more in the home country where it is produced but the same device would cost lesser to produce in countries from where they are exported.

To counter this, make domestic production competitive vis–à–vis imports, and create a commercial level playing field for domestic manufacturer, one of the tools that has been developed and one which NITI Aayog and the GoI have given the green signal to is the PLI scheme.

This innovative production-linked financial incentive has been proposed to boost domestic manufacturing and attract large investments in key priority target medical devices segments. PLI is expected to significantly make domestic manufacturing commercially competitive and will also help domestic companies gain bigger foothold while limiting imports.

With an objective to boost domestic manufacturing and attract large investment in medical device sector, the Department of Pharmaceuticals has recently launched the PLI scheme with a total financial outlay of ₹3,420 crore (approximately, $0.5 billion), for the period of five years, with the base year for sales as 2022–23.[13] The applications

---

[13]'Scheme for Promotion of Medical Device Parks.' *The Gazette of India*, Department of Pharmaceuticals, Ministry of Chemicals and Fertilizers, 21 July 2020, https://pharmaceuticals.gov.in/sites/default/

under the four priority target segments include cancer care/radiotherapy medical devices, radiology and imaging medical devices (both ionizing and non-ionizing radiation products) and nuclear imaging devices, anaesthetics and cardio-respiratory medical devices, including catheters of cardio-respiratory category and renal care medical devices, and all implants including implantable electronic devices.

The PLI scheme gives eligible manufacturing companies a five per cent incentive on incremental sales over the base year for a five-year period. The scheme has been well-received and has attracted many successful applications, which are expected to boost domestic manufacturing of medical devices over the next five to 10 years, including the ancillary industries.

ii. Phased manufacturing programme (PMP): In another effort to boost local manufacturing of parts and components of electronic medical devices, the Ministry of Electronics and Information Technology (MeitY), under the GoI, conceptualized what is known as the phased manufacturing programme (PMP). It aims to promote indigenous manufacturing and domestic value addition in locally manufactured medical devices.

files/Gazette%20notification%20of%20Medical%20Device%20schemes_1.pdf. Accessed on 23 December 2021.

Under this programme, the basic customs duty of key components is increased in a gradual manner over three to five years. A predictive increase in customs duties of key components sends a positive signal to the industry, encouraging them to make substantial efforts towards indigenization and counter the possibility of the increased cost of production. This is done in a very calibrated, consistent and predictable manner with substantial industry consultations. An exercise of this nature was successfully completed for medical X-ray machines and related products.

iii. Public procurement order (PPO): The success of manufacturing lies in market access. Given that the market for healthcare products includes both private as well as public hospitals, it is necessary to encourage markets to suitably provide opportunities to domestically-produced medical devices.

Preferential market access is a tool often used in international trade and domestic public procurement to address concerns about the balance of payment deficit and encourage local manufacturing.

It is not only the emerging economies that take recourse to this measure. The US had announced the American Recovery and Reinvestment Act in 2009, which included the 'Buy American' provision. According to this provision, funds used for construction, alteration, maintenance or repair of public buildings and public works must procure all iron, steel and manufactured goods produced only in the US, with a price preference of 25 per cent. The European Union (EU) and Canada have also adopted the preferential market access from time to time. The World Trade Organization (WTO) also does not discourage countries from developing policies to promote domestic manufacturing. Recognizing the role of government procurement in national policy, the General Agreement on Tariffs and Trade (GATT) Article III 8(a) permits governments to buy domestic products preferentially.

However, this approach requires a national structure that is systematic and transparent. The Department for Promotion of Industry and Internal Trade (DPIIT), under the Indian government, issued a PPO on these lines to provide preference to domestically produced goods by Indian or foreign companies, whose goods have 25 per cent or more local content or value addition.[14] Being

---

[14]'Public Procurement (Preference to Make in India)', Department for Promotion of Industry and Internal Trade, 15 June 2017, https://dpiit.gov.in/sites/default/files/PPP-MII-ORDER-2017_15062018_0.pdf. Accessed on 23 December 2021.

transparent and progressive, the DPIIT's order does not discriminate against foreign companies. Rather, it encourages them to add local value and take advantage of the order's provisions. Such policy intervention and incentivization would create a much-needed level playing field for domestic manufacturers who have been historically subjected to unsubstantiated preferences for imported products/technologies. Based on the PPO from DPIIT, respective line ministries issued sector-specific orders such as that issued by the Department of Pharmaceuticals, GoI, on the public procurement order for medical devices. It has a structured approach; transparent framework for benefits depending upon the percentage of value addition and appeals for compliance and query redressal.

In conclusion, the three policies explained above form an integrated approach that allows business, science and market access to progress in a comprehensive and collaborative manner. While PLI allows for incentives to be reinvested into product improvement and research, PMP provides for a gradual upgrade to the technology value chain and PPO allows for sufficient market access to get the technology and business engine going.

Over the years, I have remained closely associated with the formulation of each of these schemes and frameworks. As the chairperson of the scheme drafting committee for the PLI Scheme for Medical Devices, as a member of the committee for the PMP programme for specialized products like X-rays and as a member of the appeals committee under the PPO; I have witnessed the extensive impact these frameworks can create on the growth of a sector, the immense benefit of these to the patients at large. It is clearly and positively evident. Many of these frameworks have played a catalytic role in supporting the research and infrastructural progress we have made and continue to make in clusters like the AMTZ.

4

INDIGO FINAL CALL...TO THE CITY OF DESTINY!

It was 22 February 2016 at 5.30 a.m. at Terminal 1 of the Indira Gandhi International Airport in Delhi. A band of people with dreams in their eyes headed towards the boarding gate to catch a flight to the city of destiny, Vishakhapatnam or Vizag, as it is better known as—a city which is the headquarters of the Eastern Naval Command of the Indian Navy. It is also home to a large number of public sector enterprises such as the Gas Authority of India Limited (GAIL), the

National Thermal Power Corporation Limited (NTPC), the Hindustan Petroleum Corporation Limited (HPCL), Indian Oil and so on. It also has a strong academic culture, something that is much-needed for medical technology enterprises to grow, particularly in R&D. No wonder Sir C.V. Raman—the Noble laureate and discoverer of the Raman Effect, was once a student in this city. It was one of the cities on my radar to set up India's first medical technology park. Besides a strong academic culture, it has a large shipping port, logistics hub and also boasts refreshing beaches, a garland of mountains sometimes covered with low clouds, a lifestyle that allows creative thinking and, of course, some of the best cuisines. The group travelling with me this time to Vizag was a set of potential investors joining me on the task to find an appropriate location to set up the park.

The decision to select the final location depended on factors such as radiation protection, accessibility, distance from the port and the airport, and a myriad of other practical factors. By 10.00 a.m., we had hit the road after a quick breakfast at the Novotel next to the beach, overlooking the vast sea. After visiting a few locations, a local official urged us to head towards an area behind the famous Vizag Steel Plant. There wasn't a road leading to it or even a telephone signal. As we approached the nearly 1.2 million square metres large land, we realized that it had a spectacular setting. On one side was a chain of mountains guarding and mystically beautifying the location and on the other side, one could see the tall chimneys and heavy-duty grids of the NTPC and the steel plant in the distance. Nature on one side and engineering on the other. As we left the place, we knew this was the best location, out of the three that we had covered in our visit, for our vision to become a reality. It was situated close to the airport and the highway, although there was no approach road, water pipeline, power grid or even a PIN code. But all that was to be built as part of the park anyway if we decided to get started at the location that we found appropriate for the project.

The government was quick to approve the project. I had, by then, drafted the memorandum of association of a private limited company and a company secretary was tasked to get the formalities of registration completed. On 30 April 2016, a copy of the company registration certificate with the name 'AP MedTech Zone Limited' was in my hand and the AMTZ was born in a silent and affirmative style. There were no precedents of such an entity that dealt with the manufacturing of medical equipment which could work with private sector entities. While the Indian Institutes of Technology (IITs) that undertake research on physics and electronics are academic institutes, partnering with academic centres and private sector entities for manufacturing was a unique mandate for the AMTZ. We created a board of directors for the company that consisted of then health secretary to the government of Andhra Pradesh (AP)—an honest and sincere individual—Mrs Poonam, and five other directors, including myself, then in that capacity of an advisor (health) to the government of AP. Immediate action was required on the ground and the moment needed to be seized in the name of progress to script history for India. In a rather unusual turn of events, while still heading the health technology vertical at the NHSRC, I was appointed as the chief executive officer (CEO) of the AMTZ. The first board meeting followed soon with Mr Ravi Capoor, then joint secretary for the Ministry of Commerce and Industry, joining us for the meeting as the representative of the GoI. Mr Capoor later became the secretary for the Ministry of Textiles. Those who have had the pleasure to work with him remember him as a fair administrator and an extremely proactive professional. If you were to attend a meeting with him, a timeline for the task completion was an inevitable outcome.

While establishing the board of directors, I had the privilege of including a few other distinguished individuals. An extremely dependable person among them was Mr Sudhanshu Pandey. He is magnificent person who later became the secretary for the Department of Food and Public Distribution, GoI. A gentleman to his core, with an emphasis on the word 'gentle', Mr Sudhansh Pant, who later served as joint secretary in the MoHFW, was another addition. Mr Rajneesh Tingle and Ms Ritu Dhillon were representatives of the Department of Pharmaceuticals, GoI, who graced our board during their respective stints in an ex-officio capacity. Additionally, support also came from Mr Sanjay Chadda, a well-known, efficient administrator posted as an additional secretary with the Ministry of Commerce and Industry, GoI. Dr Madhur Gupta, the technical officer for health products at the WHO country office for India. Scientific inputs were of utmost importance and over-representation of bureaucratic strength sometimes allows technological merits to get overlooked. I decided to propose a list of a few notable scientific minds to be on the board as independent directors. Prof. M.K. Surappa, the ex-director of IIT, Ropar, and then dean of the Indian Institute of Science, Bangalore, Prof. D.S. Nagesh—a brilliant scientist at Sree

Chitra Institute, Trivandrum, and Prof. B. Ravi, professor and entrepreneur in his own right from IIT, Bombay, became directors in due course of time. I also had the pleasure of having Mr Vivek Seigell, senior director of the Progress Harmony Development (PHD) Chambers of Commerce and Industry as an industry representative. It was, perhaps, for the first time that a representative an association to the industry was on the board of a public sector enterprise. Rajiv Nath, the forum coordinator of AIMED, remained a facilitator, helping the AMTZ all along. We joked that he spent more time for the Indian medical device industry association helping brand India fly high than spending time at his factory, which produces the world-famous Dispovan syringes.

With the board of directors already having met for the first time, the land having given by the Department of Revenue, government of AP, for the project and a CEO in the chair (who spent half the week working in Delhi), it was time to lay the foundation stone. We selected 19 August 2016 for this purpose. As the day neared, we realized that all we had was an empty plot of land—more a bushy jungle, a rented office in the city of Vizag and a huge iron gate at the entrance of the plot, which primarily served to keep stray animals away. It was only on 22 December 2016 that I was relieved from my responsibilities in New Delhi. I moved to Vizag permanently on 4 January 2017 so as to take the project forward. It took exactly a year to finalize the architectural plans, obtain environmental clearance, plan and design the laboratories and draft specifications for thousands of equipment that would be used in these industrial-scale laboratories. One year was indeed a short time for all that we managed to achieve. On 3 January 2018, exactly one year to the day I had arrived in Vizag, we started the construction of the AMTZ—a name now synonymous with medical technology.

5

'IF YOU BUILD IT, THEY WILL COME'

'If you build it, they will come.' This is a famous line from the 1989 film *Field of Dreams*. For the right occupants to come, the right facilities need to be built. On 3 January 2018, our makeshift office was a collection of shipping containers at a location that did not even have cell phone network coverage. Clearly, this wasn't a very lucrative location for managers, but that's exactly the situation wherein scientists thrive. An excavator was ready to dig deep to pull out the soil to lay the first column of the initial structure—which was to be the first building of the Medical Technology Zone. The container office, as we called it, was abuzz with activity. A workforce of about 200 engineers and architects was committed to building a mini-city in the 3 million square feet area within 342 days. Each 24-hour-long day required a construction speed of about 190 square feet per minute—which was hitherto unheard of. There were clear-cut timelines for the completion of the construction of each factory and the scientific laboratories, as well. The first building scheduled to be completed was PIVOT—to house the administrative office of the AMTZ and that of the Kalam Institute of Health Technology. It was scheduled to be ready for functioning in 113 days. Just to make the situation more non-compromising for my architects and engineers, Prof. VijayRaghavan, a father figure in the scientific circles and the principal scientific advisor to the GoI, consented to fly down to the AMTZ on 30 April to hold a meeting of senior medical technologists from IITs and other distinguished organizations from across the country. A building to house the brain of the AMTZ—for a battalion of medical technologists—could not have been built faster. With footing and concrete pedestals erected in record time, the roof was cast within a record 60 days and the floors were made ready in 100 days! Most importantly, given that the technology development work on many products had already begun in the containers, it was structure following the function; unlike in many projects, where first the structure is built and then the work begins. The first national meeting at the AMTZ took place the day that the building was declared open and fit for use. A celebratory lunch was held in the corridors of the new building. A sweet personality by name of 'Chinna', who was a driver for the AMTZ team had, by then, taken the formidable responsibility of getting piping hot tea and fruits for the visitors from the nearby forest.

As buildings that constituted the AMTZ continued to be erected, there were many instances where only nature's kindness could have helped us. In one instance, as the concrete roof slab that required non-stop pouring of the concrete mix for 36 hours and covered over 80,000 square feet was being laid over the electromagnetic testing centre, a deafening clap of thunder rang out above us. Within no time, dark clouds had gathered and the weather had changed. With an enormous amount of concrete mix ready and thousands of workers waiting to begin pouring the concrete work, there was no option but to go ahead despite the stormy weather. Had it rained, it would have posed a substantial challenge—both in terms of the completion of the project within the timeline as well as the financial implications of a huge amount of concrete mix getting wasted. I was on the first floor of our office building. Looking at the mountains, I wished for us to be saved or spared from the rain. We, the immigrants in the lap of this valley, needed to be rescued by the mountains, by some kindness or luck of nature. It was a surprise that it rained and poured all over the city but not one drop of water fell from the sky onto the AMTZ campus for the next three days. Anecdotes of this kind reassured our belief in the Supreme Nature whose benevolence we need, along with all the efforts that we make.

Quality and safety need no introduction. However, safety for the sake of record-keeping is not long; safety embedded in the ethos of work does wonders. On my way to the office one morning, I read in the newspaper that the Asian Development Bank (ADB) had agreed to finance the Vizag Chennai Industrial Corridor (VCIC) project which would have several industrial nodes along its span. I immediately booked an appointment with the ADB office in Delhi. They were kind enough to give me an opportunity to make a presentation on the AMTZ. That was in 2018 and construction was in full swing with over 1,800 people working in multiple shifts to complete the task. Later, the ADB decided to come unannounced for a surprise site visit. Nishant, the head of civil engineering and safety and a hardworking individual who played a very important role in the making of the AMTZ, came running to me. He had somehow been able to connect with a member of the ADB team via a cell phone when the team was just three kilometres away. We could have made no additional preparations and it was already 5.00 p.m. The ADB team carefully surveyed the site and when they came back, they pleasantly informed us that they would be happy to support the second phase of the project for over $16 million. One of the main reasons for this, besides the extreme technicality and comprehensive planning of the project, was that during their surprise site visit, not a single worker out of thousands working on that day was found to be without a helmet and a safety belt. This constant endeavour towards safety was ably supported by Mr Kishore Babu, the chairman of the construction agency; his extremely sincere project head with a dynamic personality, Sashidhar; and my project-monitoring team leader, the soft-spoken and diligent Shiv Kumar. Financial penalties were levied on the contractor if workers were found to be not wearing shoes, googles, head gear and safety belts if the work at hand called for the use of safety gear. Among thousands of workers who toiled tirelessly were some women from the nearby villages who worked very hard every day. When the contract for the hospitality services in the zone concluded, all of them, who had earlier worked as labourers, were employed as housekeeping staff. Now wearing a clean uniform, working in air-conditioned offices and laboratories and commuting to the AMTZ campus on an electric bike, Devi, one such worker among many, symbolizes the enormous social good that projects like the AMTZ are capable of!

While I remained busy during the construction, with multiple site visits to various centres being built within the campus and scientific equipment planning, my colleagues in the newly formed but small team of Nitin Bharadwaj, Geetha Varalakshmi, Rohit Chhabra, Vamsi Krishna and a few others, kept the boat rocking and completed the various organizational administrative works with better outcomes every day. Every single concrete slab cast on the roof was celebrated, every single milestone was appreciated and every single delay was flagged for immediate course correction. It was quite difficult to source the huge amount of various construction material from within the city of Vizag. The

piles, glass, lights—in humongous quantities—were to
be brought in for the mammoth construction. Kishore
Babu and his team worked tirelessly to arrange the
supplies from Rajasthan, West Bengal, Maharashtra and
other cities like Hyderabad and Bangalore. The time was
critical and quality was of the essence. We did have the
usual scuffles between the construction team and the
project monitoring team. But every time we hit a wall,
the management leadership of all concerned entities—
including Nitin, Nishant and I from AMTZ, Kishore Babu
from the construction agency and Upendra Rao from
the project monitoring team—met on-site, resolved the
issues at hand, and realigned our resources and energies
towards better plans and outcomes. I was always amazed
by how Upendra Rao could control his panic and anger
at the errors and constantly pushed his team, which
was led by Shiv Kumar and Swati, to be more vigilant
towards achieving project timelines. Mrs Poonam, then
health secretary in the state and known to be an honest
and hardworking professional, was always there to add
support from the governance perspective.

Mr Naresh, who was an entrepreneur, activist,
industry leader and a spiritual aspirant all rolled into
one, housed us in his building in the city free of cost for
the entire year of 2017. This is when we were engaged

in planning the project specifics of the AMTZ campus before construction began in 2018. We cannot thank him enough for this gesture. This individual, without any ulterior motive, allowed us the use of a beautiful hall as a temporary office in the city. He even made sure that my staff got lunch free of cost every day along with the staff of his IT firm, who were housed in another part of the hall. His commitment to the city's development is remarkable and his enthusiasm, infectious.

The first board meeting of the AMTZ took place in Vijayawada when the AMTZ did not yet have any premises. The second one took place in the temporary offices that we had had in Vizag. The third one was in the container office on the bare plot of land allotted for the AMTZ. The next one was on the ground floor of the PIVOT building. And the fifth board meeting was convened in the newly constructed Bhabha boardroom. The board members simply could not believe the progress they saw in every subsequent meeting. Mr Sudhanshu Pandey, an extremely agile administrator himself, complimented me once saying that I was trying to build a scientific city for medical equipment in 342 days when it is otherwise difficult to even build a boundary wall in as much time for such a large, 270-acre campus. Soon, we moved into our own building on the Zone campus.

The whole concept of the AMTZ rested on the principle that if scientific infrastructure, at par with the best in the world, could be made available to our entrepreneurs, it would help them leapfrog into the orbit of complex science and product development. The next step was to give them a pristine production space, nested within several technology centres and the required instrumentation. Globally, there was no single institution that combined these facilities all in one place. The nature of the equipment, the quality control process and the architecture was all too guarded as well. Previously, I had worked on documenting such facilities in several parts of the world including the US, Germany, Singapore, Japan and China. However, I found scientific infrastructure scattered and while each of them was excellent in their own right, the consolidation of all of them in one single cluster or campus was missing. Wondering at the power of consolidation, I planned for almost every laboratory and industrial centres needed for the various categories of medical equipment, most of which came in handy at the mass-production scale during the COVID-19 crisis. While more of this has been discussed in the later chapters, let me walk you through some of the monumental centres that were built and equipped in the Zone.

1. ADDIT: Centre for 3D Printing

3D printing, also known as additive manufacturing in the machining world, is a new entrant. Using 3D printing for complex machinery is an art as well as a science. Building a mass-production centre for 3D printing was inevitable if we were to address futuristic technology as is the case in medical science. The first facility, therefore, in the plan was a mega-centre with over 100 gigantic instruments for 3D printing, additive and subtractive manufacturing.

ADDIT, as is the name of one of the world's largest 3D printing centres at the AMTZ. It was built in 184 days and equipped gradually to support a wide variety of manufacturing. Low-volume, high-precision batch production and high-volume, low-cost manufacturing became a real possibility. Rajsekhar, an engineer and entrepreneur passionate about 3D printing as a science, leads this centre along with his team from Think 3D, adding enormous value to the AMTZ ecosystem. With the support of the two brilliant minds of Avinash and Krishnakant, this centre soon became truly world-class—a house of replicating complex parts of many an equipment, including medical equipment and other industry verticals, such as aviation, robotics and defence products manufacturing.

2. BIOME: Centre for Biomaterial Testing

Once a medical device, for example, a knee implant, is 3D printed, the product would need to undergo several validation and safety studies, from chemical characterization, tensile strength measurements, electron microscopy to many other biological, biochemical and bio-engineering processes. BIOME engages in the physio-chemical and biological evaluation of samples and primarily caters to the medical device industry for all biomaterial processes required for innovations, innovative materials and product development. Supported by B.S. Ravindra and Dr Prasad and the team from TÜV Rheinland, this centre is a one of its kind where one may find a spectrum of instrumentation such as transmission electron microscope (TEM), single electron microscope (SEM), Raman spectrophotometer, confocal microscope, micro-CT for instruments, humidity-integrity-altitude-temperature chambers and other coveted instrumentation. A team of senior scientists consisting of Dilip and Santosh from the AMTZ, coordinate the activities of this centre, which is truly a landmark facility.

3. ELECTRA: Centre for EMI-EMC and Electrical Safety

Electromagnetic Interference and electromagnetic compatibility (EMI-EMC) is the core of all electronic products and a quality check for medical equipment that cannot be compromised upon. Broadly, the EMI-EMC checks for radiated emission, radiated susceptibility, conducted emission and conducted susceptibility. It is a fact that medical devices work in a very complex hospital environment and in proximity of multiple other machines and power sources. In simple terms, the EMI-EMC means the ability of a machine to protect itself from electric and electro-magnetic influences of surrounding environment. This is a life-saving characteristic in a medical device. Consider the example of an individual implanted with a pacemaker being protected from the electrical influences of the refrigerator motor while opening a fridge door at home or medical equipment being used on a person inside an ambulance being protected from vehicle engine or an electrical transformer, while the ambulance is moving on the road. Various other safety tests done in the ELECTRA Centre include electrostatic discharge testing (ESD) and ingress protection, besides testing and validation of products over a wide range of engineering safety standards. Kalyan Verma, Venkat, Santosh, Abdul and their teams consisting of brilliant engineers were assigned the task of setting up ELECTRA—indeed an 'electrifying' facility. This centre is also one of the world's largest centres to have a 10-meter chamber, 40 gigahertz (GHz), dual-mast antenna, with a six-meter wide testing table diameter and a six-ton loading capacity. It is capable of testing an ambulance, an MRI or cath lab along with every possible electro-medical equipment for international standards such as the International Electrotechnical Commission (IEC) 60601-1 and IEC-60601-1-2; which are globally harmonized packages of over 8,000 complex tests. A validation at this centre is a credible pathway which could lead to regulatory approvals from agencies such as the Conformité Européene (CE) in the EU, the Food and Drug Administration (FDA) in the US, and other such harmonized regulatory approvals globally.

4. DECIBLE: Centre for Acoustics and Wireless Testing

Noise from machines remains an important factor affecting efficiency. In the case of medical equipment that has alarms for critical clinical values, it is also an important life-saving feature. Similarly, the integration of wireless technology in healthcare, particularly in products like vital monitoring devices, is important. The Centre for Acoustics and Wireless Testing remains a vital laboratory, in addition to those at ELECTRA. This centre has the capability to provide complete sound testing, alarm measurements, noise-cancelling and looks very futuristic, almost like it could be the set for one of the movies from the *Star Wars* franchise.

5. TEXTURA: Medical Textiles That Save Lives

When a patient sees a surgeon in a gown, with a mask on their face and ready to conduct a surgical operation, the patient rarely realizes that the gown, mask, drape and head cover are all part of several layers of protection from infection that the doctors and the hospital staff offer to the patient and care providers and are not mere clinical protocols. The protective role of medical textiles became popular and recognized by the general public only during the recent pandemic. There is a huge demand for N95 masks, PPE gowns/coveralls and surgical masks that have now become part of our daily life. Such demands also increase the requirements of quality and standards check on these products. A few laboratories for masks and some for PPEs did come up in 2020 in the wake of first wave of COVID-19; however, there were no laboratories in India that could test all categories of medical textiles which range from respirators, gowns, drapes to N95 masks. It was in this hour of need that an all-inclusive medical textiles testing laboratory, TEXTURA, was set up at the AMTZ. Listed by the Bureau of Indian Standards, it is the only laboratory in India that provides testing for the entire bandwidth of textile standards such as bacterial filtration, viral filtration, breathability, clogging test and tensile strength tests. Dilip, a trusted scientific mind at the AMTZ, leads the activities of this centre.

6. COBALTA: Gamma Irradiation for Safest Sterilization

COBALTA is a prerequisite facility for international business and regulatory compliance of products that require sterilization. Whether it is a nasal swab used for COVID-19 sample collection or a dialyser used in renal dialysis or knee or hip implants, the process of gamma irradiation is considered a benchmark. The Gamma Irradiation Centre uses the radioisotope cobalt-60 to penetrate the package without opening it. This process removes all sources of infection and improves the longevity/shelf life of perishable and medical products. Housed in an extremely complex infrastructure with a 2.2-metres-thick wall of concrete and the cobalt-60 stored like shining diamonds eight meters underwater, this is an extremely risky and complex setup. The cobalt-60 produces gamma rays in a controlled manner and hence, the process is called gamma irradiation. The name given to the gamma irradiation facility at the AMTZ is COBALTA. It is dedicated to sterilizing medical devices, making it the only Gamma Irradiation Centre in the country exclusively for medical devices. Besides supporting other product lines such as food, this is among the few such facilities in India and the first in surrounding southeastern India. Supervised by a dedicated engineer—Deepak and his team working round the clock, this facility has been set up as per strict safety and regulatory supervision of the Atomic Energy Regulatory Board (AERB). The facility caters to a large category of medical devices, implants and life-saving products.

7. MEDI-VALLEY: Incubating the dreamers

MEDI-VALLEY, the innovation arm of the AMTZ, is an Atal Incubation Centre supported by the NITI Aayog under the Atal Innovation Mission (AIM). NITI Aayog is the highest policy support institution in the country, and AIM is a state-of-the-art incubator dedicated to health technology and located within the medical devices manufacturing epicenter, MEDI-VALLEY provides technical mentorship by stalwart researchers, technology and innovation champions and leading manufacturers. MEDI-VALLEY trains the innovators along all stages, from ideation to manufacturing. Medical technology innovation is a multidisciplinary approach encompassing aspects of several fields of science and engineering. MEDI-VALLEY has established its own state-of-the-art laboratory facilities where innovators can tinker with their ideas in all domains of biomedical engineering. The core MEDI-VALLEY facility covers 22,000 square feet of co-working space for laboratories, offices, meetings, and co-habitation of ideas. Under the leadership of Dr Anand Krishnan, a scientist with decades of experience in the advanced engineering systems of the United Kingdom, MEDI-VALLEY has provided support to over 40 start-ups directly and has encouraged many more budding enterprises through its pioneering knowledge-base and laboratory support within two short years. MEDI-VALLEY bears the entire cost of the first batch of prototypes, testing services and potential market access support, thus creating a structured runway from which the dreams of young entrepreneurs can take off. MEDI-VALLEY has been a support platform for small and medium-scale enterprises from across the country for providing critical testing and rapid prototyping services for oxygen concentrators, ventilators, BiPAP, CPAP and several other cardio-pulmonary devices, particularly during the COVID-19 pandemic.

8. BIO-VALLEY: Where Biology Meets Engineering

BIO-VALLEY is yet another specialized incubator supported by the Biotechnology Industry Research Assistance Council (BIRAC), a programmatic institution under the aegis of the Department of Biotechnology (DBT), GoI. It has been set up to foster complex and hybrid technologies which integrate medical engineering with biophysics, genetics, electronics and cellular biology. BIO-VALLEY specializes in converging technological principles providing unlimited access to cutting-edge product research, as well as market access support.

It ensures that the right blend of expert mentorship, access to venture funding, R&D facilitation, testing infrastructure and industry collaboration is provided. Led by Dilip Kumar, BIO-VALLEY contributes in a big way to the indigenization of components for in-vitro diagnostics, exosome research and has been at the forefront of the production of RT-PCR kits for COVID-19 supplies.

9. GALAXY: Laser Centre for Advanced Optics

GALAXY (Global Application of Lasers and Auxiliary Sciences) is a state-of-the-art laser centre with high-power femto-second lasers that perform optical testing, research, promote innovation in medical lasers, microfluidics and biophotonics. Testing the laser devices like ophthalmoscopes, laser scalpels, photobiomodulation devices (low-level laser therapy), dental and dermatological lasers, photometry devices, X-ray machines, surgical microscope for the eye and gastroscopes are some of the complex medical devices GALAXY can support. Collaborating to create cutting-edge innovations in the field of biophotonic and biomedical applications, the use of optics and light in medicine aiming for higher accuracy and precision are key objectives of GALAXY. GALAXY works under the magic of Santosh, a specialist in optoelectronics. With a myriad of medical applications, from diagnostics to therapeutics to surgical procedures with light generation, focusing on manipulation and detection, GALAXY adds a phenomenal value and complements the rest of the medical ecosystem at the AMTZ. Equipped with high-end optical equipment like a femto-second laser, auto-correlators, dispersion compensating optics and wide-range measurement devices from Ophir Photonics to monitor the critical laser parameters, GALAXY is a versatile testing and research centre that brings out cutting-edge innovations in the fields of surface enhanced Raman Spectroscopy for detecting and ablating cancer cells, diffuse optics, fluorescence spectroscopy, optofluidic applications and several other medical imaging and diagnostic technologies such as thermal imaging, ultrasound machines, laser welding for in-vitro diagnostics, endoscopes and fundus cameras.

10. SILICO: Centre for Electronic Components and Sensors

Printed circuit board (PCB) assembly has become critically important in the MedTech domain, and the range of PCB

Construction of the AMTZ begins in early January 2018.

'If you build it, they will come': Overseeing the construction work.

With Prof. K. VijayRaghavan (left), principal scientific adviser to the Government of India, at the construction site.

COBALTA, the Center for Gamma Irradiation with cobalt-60, under construction.

COBALTA is now the pride of the AMTZ.

The pace of development in modern India—the AMTZ office was built in 113 days.

I HUB
World Incubation Hub

I-Hub: A world stage for innovation.

All set to install the national flag on the premises.

The Tricolour stands tall at 108 feet.

In conversation with former Indian Test cricketer, Virender Sehwag (right) at the Fourth WHO Global Forum on Medical Devices, the World Cup of MedTech was held in India for the first time in 2018.

Dr V.K. Paul, member, NITI Aayog, speaks at the Fourth WHO Global Forum on Medical Devices at the AMTZ in 2018.

Over 1500 delegates from more than 100 countries celebrate the birth of the AMTZ at the Fourth WHO Global Forum on Medical Devices in 2018.

The AMTZ board of directors in 2018 (from left): Vivek Seigell, Dr. Poonam Malakondaiah, Sudhanshu Pandey and the author, Dr J.K. Sharma.

From making masks to MRI machines, the AMTZ is the largest MedTech cluster globally.

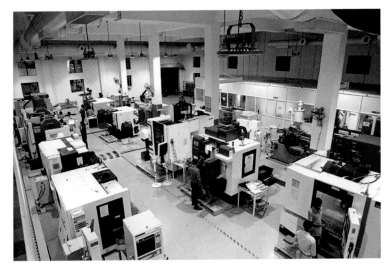

The AMTZ leads by example: Common scientific facilities for industry.

The world's largest IVD cluster at the AMTZ making a million RT-PCR kits a day.

Moulding centres: Where large-scale manufacturing becomes a reality.

Tens of thousands of ventilators waiting to be shipped across the country.

Life-saving oxygen concentrators being assembled.

Over 20,000 oxygen concentrators supplied.

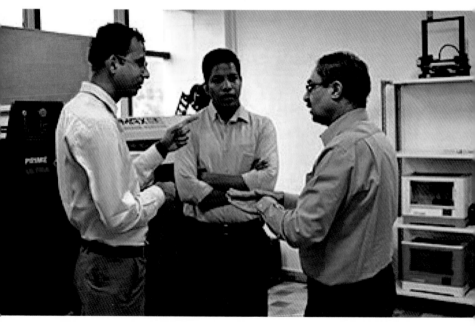

Fuelling innovation through economical prototyping: At the largest 3D facility of the world with Ajay Sawhney (extreme right), secretary, Ministry of Electronics and Information Technology (MeitY).

With the Hon. Barry O'Farrell (third from right) AO, Australia's high commissioner to India and ambassador to Bhutan.

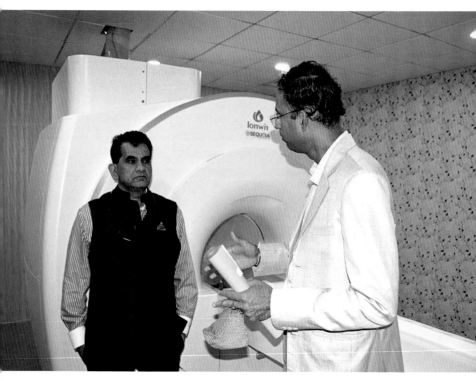

Amitabh Kant (left), CEO, NITI Aayog with India's first MRI superconducting magnet.

applications in the medical field is vast and ever-growing. Medical PCBs are fitted in everything from defibrillators and heart monitors in the case of cardiovascular medical devices to medical imaging systems, MRIs, CT scans, ultrasonic equipment, and simple instruments such as temperature monitors and blood glucose monitors. To cater to the needs of manufacturers with the complex assembly of surface mount devices/components onto the PCBs, a fully automatic PCB assembly and sensor facility was called SILICO was set up at the AMTZ. Besides the PCB line, SILICO includes a solder paste printer and a 3D inspection system to meet the quality standards, a flexible pick-and-place machine with a capacity of up to 45,000 components per hour (CPH), a reflow oven with eight zones and an automated optical inspection system that provide real-time pass/fail analysis of defects for the final quality inspection. By creating a box-build assembly with design capabilities for manufacturing and assembly in-house, the lead time for manufacturers for getting subassemblies of PCBs is reduced. This creates value addition to the manufacturers in the zone as well. Sensor lines for oxygen sensors and flow sensors, among other critical components, add tremendous value to this facility. Operated by an internationally renowned firm—Amphenol, this facility is critical to the medical equipment manufacturing ecosystem at the AMTZ. And yes, both the facility and Junaid, our brilliant scientist in charge of this centre, work with precision and professionalism par excellence.

11. DIODE: Superconducting Magnet Centre

While we all are generally aware of the magnetic resonance imaging system that is extensively used in neurological, orthopaedic and other applications. An MRI system is made up of over 20 complex subsystems comprising thousands of small and large components. Most complicated among them is the superconducting magnet, which makes up over 60 per cent of the cost of the materials used in an MRI. There are very few places in the world that can boast a superconducting magnet manufacturing facility for MRI applications.

In a specialized facility sprawling over 50,000 square feet, the AMTZ houses a centre named DIODE, an internationally benchmarked infrastructure with a well-equipped assembly line for superconducting magnets, 10 ton EOT crane, helium liquefication systems, helium mass spectrometers, cryocoolers and radio-frequency shielded (RF) cages (also called Faraday cages) equipped with tesla meters for testing and fine-tuning the magnets and is capable of producing superconducting magnets of multiple configurations including 1.5 tesla and 3 tesla. Operated in partnership with Jansen India, this facility is quickly emerging as a gateway for MRI production in India. Very often, one may find, our engineer in charge of this centre, Krishnakant—wearing a big smile, hovering around the centre.

12. OXY-ZONE: Oxygen Is Life!

The OXY-ZONE Centre is a cryogenic air separation unit that can generate oxygen for medical-grade requirements like the EMS (Emergency Medical Services), ambulance applications, but most importantly, for use in the various manufacturing processes. During the COVID-19 pandemic, the oxygen demand was substantial not only in hospitals treating the infected patients but also the manufacturers of ventilators and other essential products that needed oxygen to perform quality assurance/quality control processes, metal sheet fabrication, along with the many products that needed nitrogen. OXY-ZONE helped supply enough oxygen to perform these activities. The plant has an inbuilt cylinder-filling capability to fill the high-capacity cylinders at 150bar/2,200 psi pressure. It can fill up to 300 cylinders or 2,400 cubic metres of oxygen every day, sufficient for manufacturing units at the AMTZ and nearby hospitals. The process of oxygen and nitrogen generation starts with intake of filtered air into the compressor. Then the compressed air is cooled and pumped into a moisture separator and a cascade cooler. It is then sent into several chambers such as carbon tank, dust filter, adsorber and molecular sieve battery and finally sent to an air separation unit (ASU) which uses multi-column cryogenic distillation process to produce gaseous oxygen and nitrogen. This facility is critical to the vital manufacturing processes and also supplies the neighbouring hospitals in the region.

13. TECHTRON: Radio-isotope Generation Centre

TECHTRON is a medical cyclotron facility at the AMTZ that produces radioisotopes essential for nuclear imaging. The PET radiotracer routinely produced all over the world in medical cyclotrons is fluorine-18 (^{18}F). Approximately 30Ci (Curie) of fluorine-18 can be produced in just two hours of irradiation from which 20Ci of final FDG is synthesized, tested for quality, and, finally, released for commercial supply. ^{18}F-FDG is the workhorse in PET centres for cancer staging, assessing the spread of cancer in the body, treatment response, brain diseases and heart viability. ^{18}F has a half-life of just 110 minutes. Hence, it requires rapid transport after production. While several other molecules like ^{18}F-Dopa, ^{18}F-PSMA, can also be prepared in this facility, the facility has been created to produce other advanced radioisotopes such as iodine-131 and molybdenum-99. The facility consists of a cyclotron room, synthesis lab with automatic chemistry synthesis modules, automatic dispensing systems quality control lab with thin layer chromatography, multichannel analyser, packaging and dispatch areas and a production hot-cell made of lead shielding and a stainless-steel finishing capable of handling radioactive activity. The cyclotron is a negative hydrogen (H-) type capable of accelerating H- ions and extracting proton energy of 18 MeV (megaelectronvolts), on a beam current not more than 300µA (microamperes). This model of the medical cyclotron is the first in the Indian subcontinent.

14. ORGEN: The World of Organ Generation

The ORGEN facility at the AMTZ is a one-of-a-kind 3D-bioprinting facility developed as the Centre For Biophysics to promote research and development in 3D bioprinting of grafts, tissues, organoids, organs and aid in the development of a bio-ink. The facility has a dedicated International Organization for Standardization (ISO) class 7 cell and tissue culture laboratory, an analytical laboratory, a microbiology laboratory, a blood bank set-up along with an array of world-class equipment, including the EnvisionTEC 3D-Bioplotter that allows biofabrication research in the skin, cartilage, bone, blood vessels and organs such as the heart, kidney, placenta, ovaries, etc., as well as drug and nutrient delivery. It also includes a bioreactor, liquid nitrogen containers with a capacity of 350 litres for cryopreservation and bio-3D printers for co-axial printing. The facility partners with the Translational Research Initiative for Cell Engineering and Printing (TRICEP) Centre at the University of Wollongong, Australia. Under the revolutionary leadership of Prof. Gordon Wallace and his team, TRICEP has developed bio-inks of immense medical potential. Valuable information and expertise relating to biomaterial/nanomaterial synthesis, fabrication and characterization, prototyping biomaterial applications in medical bionics developed through multiple projects and independent research from renowned educational institutions form the global network of ORGEN. This out-of-the-world centre is associated with multiple partners in developing a miniature heart made of autologous stem cells using the bioprinting technique and also the development of 3D bioprinted ears. ORGEN aims to develop at least three organs in the next three years. Additionally, the lab at the ORGEN facility acts as a platform that can partially replace testing done on animal models.

15. ARC: Animal Research Centre

Pioneering work on medical devices development requires sufficient testing on large animals such as swine, sheep and goats to ensure that a follow-up period of over three to five years provides baseline safety data on the impact of medical devices such as a pacemaker in humans over long time periods. Such analysis is essential to ensure that the implants, electronics and other high-complexity devices that are fiitted inside the human body are perfectly safe before they are produced in large numbers and given market authorization. The Animal Research Centre supported by the Indian Council of Medical Research (ICMR) at the AMTZ is perhaps the largest animal research facility in India that specializes in medical devices. Built on over 10,000 square feet of classified facility with an ISO class 7 clean room, the ARC facility includes the capacity to handle two different species of large animals in separate containment along with their respective isolation, holding and quarantine rooms. They also come with a fully equipped operation theatre, a surgery and pre-surgery room attached to a laboratory, an in-vitro laboratory, a clinical chemistry laboratory, an analytical laboratory, a histopathology laboratory with tissue processing unit and a haematology laboratory that offers complete multispecies testing capability with practical automation with high-throughput capacity. The ARC provides access to manufacturers for safety and efficacy studies, cytotoxicity testing, sensitization testing, implantation studies, genetic and systemic toxicology studies, surgical implantation studies and chemical characterization studies to name a few. The ARC at the AMTZ augments the existing efforts for the indigenous development of medical devices in India by supporting pre-clinical validation to the in-house development of medical devices as well as by providing additional capacity to the Indian medical device industry and academia for their medical device development process.

16. STERILLA: Go Clean!

Sterilization or getting the product free from infections is a critical and a life-saving step in medical devices production. Packaging and sterilization of medical devices and healthcare products not only provide logistical safety for products but also quality assurance. Sterilizing the products individually during the manufacturing process is both technically and financially effortful. STERILLA provides a one-stop solution in an ISO class 8 clean room facility for packaging and ethylene oxide (ETO) sterilization of medical, pharmaceutical, healthcare and food products as per regulatory guidelines. This reduces the bioburden of the products as ethylene oxide causes alkylation of nucleic acids (DNA, RNA) and proteins, making the microorganisms non-viable. ETO gas can penetrate through breathable packaging, make contact with all accessible surfaces, and sterilize the product completely. The entire process of sterilization occurs at a low-temperature range of $37°C–55°C$ making it suitable for sterilizing heat-sensitive materials or products. Further, STERILLA also provides a state-of-the-art microwave sterilization chamber that is environmentally safe, resource efficient and user friendly. The disinfection is done by the microwaves generated from the magnetron source as these microwaves create a dielectric field, causing heat production leading to coagulation of structural and functional proteins of the organisms, making them non-viable. Ravi Vittal and his expert team provide the services seamlessly to all manufacturing enterprises, helping them produce safe medical products.

17. Warehouse and Logistics Hub

While medical equipment manufacturing is a scientific and complex activity, the culmination of this endeavour is only with the products reaching safely and timely to the places of their use such as hospitals and patients. This requires robust and dependable storage. Coordinated by an experienced AMTZ staff member, Manish Rastogi, in partnership with Balmer Lawrie & Co. Ltd, a very respected public enterprise, the Warehouse and Logistics Hub is a facility equalling the size of at least two football fields, committed to cater to the storage and logistical needs of all manufacturing partners at the AMTZ. This hub is spread over an area of three acres. It has a volumetric space capacity of millions of cubic feet, including two cold storage mega chambers and 500 tons of modular capacity pallet racking system, manned and cyber security systems, and is integrated with a rapid logistics network. This mega facility offers a one-stop solution for maximizing space utilization of manufacturing facilities and minimizing operational costs of storage and logistics.

18. MEDI-SHORE: Customer Support Centre

Medical devices are a serious business and managing clients' expectations is quite a difficult proposition. That's simply because the impact of products is life-saving and timely redressal of maintenance and warranty issues is critical to maintaining smooth operations inside hospitals. To ensure that all partners of the AMTZ have a common gateway for registering warranty and that maintenance queries are managed efficiently, AMTZ's Customer Service Support Centre, MEDI-SHORE, works seamlessly, coordinating with thousands of biomedical engineers who provide ground support across all sites of installation for all medical equipment produced at the AMTZ. With a highly motivated team that manages digitized services, voice and non-voice process outsourcing services and delivery of result-oriented coordination with the manufacturers, time-bound communication and closure of queries and maintenance call logs, the MEDI-SHORE Centre aims to fulfil the understandably high and non-negotiable expectations every day. Besides, under the leadership of a very talented digital services expert,

Vivekanand, this centre also serves as the knowledge bank of products with quick resolution guides built into customized customer relationship management (CRM). The centre is so scalable and well-equipped that it can handle an enormous volume of queries. The toll-free number 1800 891 3009 allows no-cost calls, enabling any responsible healthcare practitioner in the thousands of hospitals and healthcare settings that we serve to request our support almost instantaneously. MEDI-SHORE has employed youth from the economically weaker section of the society and is generating employment opportunities for hundreds of them through our partners in the Rural Shores centre, a highly passionate and socially motivated enterprise.

These 18 gems stud the crown of the AMTZ, allowing it to stand in the service of the patients and the industry in a comprehensive, collaborative and complimentary partnership.

When I had first started to plan the AMTZ, we set a target to bring up four facilities of this nature; however, with the demand from enterprises, the necessity of complex processes to be integrated into one roof, and the requirements of multiple product segments, building and operationalizing all of these became necessary. Across these 18 facilities, there are over 11,000 units of high-tech instruments and equipment, serving the needs of product development, manufacturers and entrepreneurs. Besides, we also have a dedicated Bank (ICICI bank, AMTZ Campus) to provide financial services to all the occupants of the AMTZ. While it is pride to see the 'AMTZ Campus Branch' written across the cheque leaflet of the bank, one cannot help but imagine all this happening within a place, which was a bare plot of land a mere 36 months ago. As this book is being written, many more centres are being built. The Centre of Excellence for Additive Manufacturing, which will provide services of additive materials, the National Sensors Hub, where medical grade sensors will be manufactures and a Mold Bank to provide dyes and moulds for the outer casings of products, are all being put up at rocket speed—now an AMTZ way of life.

6

'THE OUTCOME OF TODAY'S MEETING IS DISCOVERING THIS MAN!'

KIHT@ 45,000 ft

The genesis of the Kalam Institute of Health Technology (KIHT) is rooted in a providentially incidental meeting. It so happened that then principal scientific advisor (PSA) to the Government of India, Dr R. Chidambaram, called for a meeting on the indigenization of the medical technology sector. Representatives of various concerned ministries were invited. I received a call from the Joint Secretary of Commerce, Mr Ravi Capoor (later, he became the first representative of the GoI on the board of the AMTZ) at 11.00 a.m., who asked if I could join the meeting at 3.00 p.m., in the Vigyan Bhavan Annexe building. In the meeting, the then secretary of the Department of Biotechnology, Prof. VijayRaghavan, a man of deep wisdom was also in attendance. I had never met him before this meeting.

Sharing my perspective on the indigenization of the medical technology sector, I only mentioned to the committee that, while every medical technology product is complex in its entirety, when we break down the product into components, we are left with two distinct categories. Category one components are sector agnostic and readily available in India because of their applications in other sectors, like simple electronic parts. For example, air compressors or light sources. The second set of components is very specialized and specific to the medical devices sector, such as oxygen sensors. What I proposed in that meeting was to create a knowledge document that established the linkages between medical devices that were not made in the country at that time and link them to the critical components that were also not manufactured locally. The hypothesis I put forth was that if we put our efforts into making the critical components specific to the medical devices sector, the manufacturing of medical devices would automatically get a revolutionary boost.

The second point that I put forth was that while academic and research institutions do valuable research, their research generally stays with them within the campus or at most, in scientific papers. Suppose we were to create an aggregator for ready-to-use technology and an e-auction portal for the outcomes of research/ intellectual properties/prototypes. In that case, these could be funneled into the industry by the transaction on the e-market place. The industry would greatly benefit from the knowledge available in academic institutions. The institution would get the cost of research reimbursed by the sale of prototypes or associated technology transfer.

These two propositions, one to identify the critical components that can give us the breakthrough in manufacturing complex devices and the second to funnel the research into the industry, were accepted as broad decisions of the historic meeting. The meeting ended with a sweet remark from Prof. VijayRaghavan: 'The outcome of today's meeting is discovering this man!' Since then, he has truly given me the affection of a father figure.

Almost immediately, I felt that the functions accepted by the committee should not be seen as a one-time exercise but a constant pathway that required to be institutionalized into full-fledged operations.

Thus, the idea of a project institute supported by the Department of Biotechnology was born. It was named the Kalam Institute of Healthcare Technology (KIHT), with the name chosen in honor and memory of late Dr A.P.J. Abdul Kalam, the people's president and scientist. Prof. VijayRaghavan assured me that he would take the proposals up within the department to get formal approvals on budget and functions.

The next day, I travelled to the WHO headquarters in Geneva for a meeting. On my flight, I kept thinking about translating the minutes of the meeting into a functional organization. With my handbag tucked into the luggage section, I requested for some paper napkins from the cabin crew and started to pen down the entire concept of the KIHT on paper napkins. Yes, the KIHT was born at an altitude of 45,000 feet, literally on paper napkins. After I was back, I formally sent the concept ahead to Prof. VijayRaghavan who corresponded it to Dr Renu Swaroop, the then managing director of BIRAC, the enterprise and innovation arm of the DBT.

Dr Renu Swaroop, a simple and well-respected technology administrator, who later succeeded Prof. VijayRaghavan as the secretary in the DBT, has remained a constant source of support to the AMTZ and the KIHT. The Kalam Institute was registered as a DBT-supported project institute and an autonomous society of the AMTZ. Its governing body then included Prof. VijayRaghavan, Dr Renu, Dr Balram Bhargava, who later became the secretary in the Department of Health Research and the director general of the ICMR, and several other technology administrators.

Gradually, from an in-house technological intelligence arm of the AMTZ, the KIHT has now been playing the role of a medical technology consultant to several states and several ministries of the GoI. KIHT was conceived as a hub of technology banking services that would act as a valuable bridge between innovators/research institutions and manufacturers. KIHT supports technology transfers and plays a key role in drafting standards for medical equipment by the Bureau of Indian Standards (BIS). As the programmme management unit for medical technology projects, KIHT provides constant inputs for policy support and programme management to various complex projects such as conceptual designing of mobile container hospitals and RT-PCR testing vehicles during the COVID-19 pandemic.

We positioned the KIHT as the knowledge destination because the AMTZ has primarily been conceived as an investment and manufacturing destination. The presence of the KIHT puts the AMTZ in a different sphere compared to any other manufacturing park globally, as the integration of a specialized knowledge institution in a manufacturing destination is both unique and highly rewarding for the sector.

Today, KIHT works as the technology transfer organization linking academia with industry, as the Health Technology Assessment Centre for the Department of Health Research, and as the Price Monitoring and Resource Unit for the National Pharmaceutical Pricing Authority (NPPA). It also works as the Joanna Briggs Centre for generating clinical evidence on medical technologies and support organizations such as the International Society for Pharmaceutical Education, Outcomes and Research (ISPOR).

It is quite providential that due to the huge knowledge base KIHT creates through its market intelligence cell and other departments, the AMTZ serves as a member of the Brazil Russia India China and South Africa (BRICS) Business Council's Working Group (Manufacturing), which consists of well-respected, legendary organizations such as, the Tata group, the Birla group, Apollo Tyres and the Mahindra group.

National Medical Devices Promotion Council

Trade is indeed the genesis of many industrial efforts. However, tariff and non-tariff barriers can facilitate or hinder industrial efforts. Early intervention of such factors is essential in helping developing sectors such as MedTech grow, guided and guarded by industrial policies that are protective yet globalized. In governance, it is, therefore, necessary to have a policy desk for such functions, which is close enough to policymaking and yet has sufficient involvement of industry members, divided by a thin line of institutional discipline. Many bodies such as the Pharmaceuticals Export Promotion Council of India (Pharmexcil), the Engineering Export Promotion Council (EEPC) and a few other organizations in other sectors perform this well-balanced role. Matters such as tracking customs duties, trade among nations from the perspective of export–import trade balance and time to gain market authorization are all important metrics to understand current progress and for estimating growth. Despite their aggressive in-house marketing and sales departments, most private enterprises do not conduct these macro assessments.

It was by sheer chance that the then minister for commerce and industries was visiting the city of Vizag to attend an investment conclave. I was quick to propose a National Medical Device Promotion Council (NMDPC), which he kindly agreed to approve. I was asked to make a presentation stating the council's objectives, purpose and functioning at a meeting called by the Ministry of Commerce in New Delhi. With the AMTZ playing a pivotal role in facilitating the formation of the council, it was set up under the aegis of the Department of Industry Policy and Promotion (DIPP), now known as the DPIIT, on 7 December 2018. Six days later, during the three-day inaugural event of the AMTZ, the NMDPC was officially launched.

The NMDPC endeavours to facilitate a continuous interaction among all stakeholders to update the understanding of industry concerns, information and certification and the regulatory and non-regulatory needs of Indian companies so as to enter global trade. It also makes recommendations to the government based on the feedback from the industry and global practices on policy and process interventions to strengthen the MedTech sector including trade interventions. Creating analytical documents for correction of inverted duty structure, to monitoring hundreds of tenders enabling fair trade, there are many best practices that the NMDPC leads today. While it is not yet a legal entity represented by the manufacturing industry, we are constantly engaged in efforts to set up an export promotion council which would allow the NMDPC to function as a distinct legal entity, led by manufacturers themselves.

The Indian Biomedical Skill Council (IBSC)

It was a casual reading of the book *Bringing the Rainbow: The Hindware Story*, India's most-respected brand for sanitary fitting, and the inspiring story of Mr R.K. Somani, the founder of Hindware, that truly deserve the credit for the genesis of the Indian Biomedical Skill Council (IBSC). One may wonder how medical technology is related to bathroom fittings!

Skill is not just a product requirement but a trade requirement in medical devices. Biomedical engineers and clinical engineers worldwide are trained in the requisite product and can work on installing, commissioning, repairing and maintaining medical devices. However, biomedical engineers trained in India cannot install or repair medical equipment in most other parts of the world. That is simply because medical equipment support and maintenance is a regulated profession in the USA, the EU, the UK, Japan and most other countries that recognize the immensely complex nature of the work of professionals who deal with medical devices.

Earlier, the availability and applicability of biomedical resources were never dealt with institutionally. Although post liberalization, the number of healthcare service providers and the gamut of medical devices grew in volumes across all segments, the demand and supply statistics of biomedical engineers remained an academic exercise. India produces close to 6,000 biomedical engineers every year but only 20–30 per cent get opportunities to work in the healthcare industry and the rest are forced to search for employment opportunities in other sectors. The industry does not seem to have been sensitized to the intrinsic value addition potential of biomedical engineers. In the absence of any accreditations or certification, biomedical engineers could neither aim for pay parity within the country nor avail the opportunities outside India.

There were two essentials to creating a globally harmonized skill accreditation structure: first, that it should have industry participation, and secondly, it must be recognized by the national skill regulator. To get the first prerequisite in place, I was in Delhi in early 2018 to meet my good friend, Anil Jauhri, the then CEO of the National Accreditation Board for Certification Bodies (NABCB) under the Quality Council of India (QCI). I, of course, requested that Mr Rajiv Nath be present as well, so that I could get his honest feedback and criticism on the proposal. It is always better to have opinions from honest and passionate people before doing something that will impact an entire sector. Rajiv Nath would also bring technical inputs as to whether the Indian medical devices manufacturing industry is rightly positioned for a skill-tech revolution. As always, Mr Jauhri's work desk was stacked with documents, so much so that I had to reach over the many files piled up on his desk to hand him the large piece of paper with complex organizations and scheme diagrams. It took less than seven minutes for both of them to see the value in the proposal. Immediately, we agreed to sign a tripartite MoU between the AMTZ, the QCI and the AIMED to set up the Indian Biomedical Skill Council. Subsequent to signing the MoU, we designed the accreditation process, the examination modalities for accrediting the applicants and discussed how we could generate awareness among professional leaders in the biomedical sector. We were fortunate that the Department of Pharmaceuticals, GoI, hosted the India Pharma & India Medical Device summit in Bengaluru in the third week of February 2018. Indeed, this was a great opportunity to bring all the stakeholders together. The first meeting of the IBSC core committee was held at the Bengaluru International Exhibition Centre on the sidelines of the India Pharma & India Medical Device summit. Mr Sudhansh Pant, a member of the board of directors of the AMTZ at that time and joint secretary in the Department of Pharmaceuticals, chaired the first meeting. With the stakeholders on board, the content of the certification process was the next milestone which needed the wisdom and time of some of the best minds in biomedical engineering. Over 70 experts and academic champions from across the country were invited to participate in this initiative. Their knowledge, discretion, and ability to converge academic knowledge with practical experience supported the creation of the core content of the certification process, including the examination questionnaire. With the entire content of the accreditation process now ready, a skill certification programme was launched for biomedical practitioners for the first time in India. However, it is necessary to have such programmes receive accreditation from the National Skill Development Agency (NSDA). Efforts were made to present the vision and the process of biomedical skill accreditation to the NSDA. After a series of very engaging and informative deliberations, on 22 August 2019, the NDSA approved five job roles pertaining to medical devices skills as proposed by the IBSC. It was a historic day. Finally, for the first time in India, the job roles pertaining to biomedical engineering were admitted under the National Skills Qualifications Framework (NSQF). This made the IBSC into a full-fledged skill council. Since then the IBSC has forged partnerships with multiple skill certification and accreditation bodies such as the Association for Advancement of Medical Instrumentation (AAMI)—a global body with its headquarters in the US.

The IBSC now provides for the certification of technical human resources in an advanced and fast-changing field such as MedTech. Thus, skill certification was put in place to support the vision of the AMTZ and 'skills', which are a major non-tariff barrier for markets, were integrated in a structured manner through internationally harmonized skill assessment programmes, providing manufacturers with the interoperability of human capital across global manufacturing sites. With time, the Department of Biotechnology's Skill Vigyan Centre was added. The Skill Vigyan Centre provides for specific training modules and courses empowering technicians, engineers and entrepreneurs. With the Skill

Vigyan Centre, prior to aiming for examination and accreditation, the applicants could now aim to get trained in management and maintenance of high-tech medical equipment. Training by the Skill Vigyan Centre and the skill accreditation by the IBSC remains a hallmark of the AMTZ's strategic response to building the medical devices sector. These trainings cover a large number of courses—complex 3D printing, biomaterials, novel approaches to innovation, entrepreneurship and health technology management.

The WHO Prequalification Cell

Quality standards applicable to various products—particularly if the products are globally exported—are highly relevant in terms of product credibility and manufacturing process standardization. While regulators of medical products look at the standards of safety and quality through the national regulatory frameworks, the products supplied through the support of the UN are required to undergo the WHO prequalification process. This process considers the product's performance, quality and safety. However, manufacturers who aim to achieve such benchmarks require an enormous amount of technical guidance, which is not always available.

In order to address this huge gap, the WHO country office for India was very keen to have the WHO prequalification support centres established across the country. Dr Madhur Gupta, a technical officer in the WHO country office for India, a member of the executive body of the Kalam Institute of Health Technology, and an extremely passionate professional, suggested that the AMTZ could apply to be one such centre.

This was the first such international outreach initiative to benchmark Indian medical devices to internationally harmonized quality safety standards. With substantial efforts of the AMTZ and WHO India office, in particular, the pivotal role played by Dr Madhur and her colleague Ms Manisha Sridhar, the WHO prequalification cell was approved on 22 November 2018, just three weeks before the WHO Global Forum was hosted at the AMTZ, Vizag, as part of the AMTZ's dedication to the nation. Since then, the WHO prequalification support centre has been playing a pivotal role in supporting manufacturers attain the highest standards of quality and safety, particularly in the domain of in-vitro diagnostics.

The four programmatic institutions, whose genesis and continued work has been recounted here, are not mere programmes. They truly stand as pillars for the medical equipment sector, enabling a unique growth story. Never before has the creation of a manufacturing park been complimented with such a comprehensive array of institutions—the creation of trade policy facilitatory systems, skill accreditation programmes and a knowledge bank dedicated to the sector. Over the past three years, many other sectoral working groups and delegations from various ministries, such as, Textiles, Machinery, Heavy Engineering and Defence Production have visited the AMTZ to savour the pace of work and witness the demonstration of a comprehensive rainbow of services, infrastructure and policies.

Truly, what makes the AMTZ very strong and unique is the combination of globally condensed knowledge brought together by Indian scientists from over 30 countries, all of whom have made the AMTZ a professional paradise—a haven of globally harmonized skill sets with globally benchmarked infrastructure.

7

'THIS IS CALLED THE AUDACITY OF HOPE!'

I knew that, broadly, the construction of the AMTZ, the world's first medical equipment park, would tentatively be completed by December 2018 as per the construction schedule. Surprisingly, while the norm is to be behind schedule, few buildings were built well ahead. Over 2,000 workers, hundreds of engineers and architects worked around the clock to accomplish the target. Approximately five kilometres of road length within the proposed campus, and about two million square feet of constructed space were under construction at an unbelievable pace. We did have a few near misses but not a single injury or fatality was caused due to any occupational hazard. Of course, there were some panic buttons, as can be imagined in any large project. In one instance, a construction worker, partly out of negligence, fell inside the large chimney of a concrete batching plant, into the well, where tons of sand and concrete are mixed. We held on to the worker using ropes and did not let him get buried in the sand, and he remained submerged up to his neck in the huge sandpit for about 30 minutes. During this time, the sand was drained in a calibrated manner, and the worker was pulled out and sent for medical care to a hospital immediately. Luckily there were no injuries, sand being a soft landing platform. The worker knew that he had just escaped a life-threatening situation and promised to be very careful while at work. He came back on duty the next day. Such was the dedication of people building the AMTZ. On 7 November 2018, the day of Diwali—the festival of lights celebrated in India and across the world—as a token of our gratitude, we gifted new clothes to each of the thousands of workers. Besides providing their work uniform, no employer had shown them this kind of affection or attempted to build and strengthen a bond with them. We are simply honoured to be getting an opportunity to be grateful.

I did wish for the inauguration of the AMTZ to be a grand event, not just by the presence of dignitaries but also by the creation of knowledge during the event. It had to create an environment that would be a mix of professional excellence, like a university; networking, like a conference; and celebration, like a grand beginning. I was wondering what that could be like! It obviously could not have been a single day's affair. It had to be spanned over a number of days according to a very structured programme that connected all partners, investors, scientists, policymakers and public representatives.

In May 2016, I was one of the delegates for the WHO Global Forum on medical devices in Geneva, a city I am very much familiar with, due to my past work with the WHO. The WHO Global Forum on medical devices had happened thrice by then, mostly in the Geneva International Conference Centre (CICG), a very spacious convention centre in the heart of the city. The spacious halls of this convention centre overlook the famous 'Broken Chair' at the entrance of the UN building in Geneva. The 'Broken Chair' is a monumental sculpture by the Swiss artist Daniel Bersef, constructed by the carpenter Louise Geneve. Constructed from 5.5

tons of wood and rising 12 metres high, it depicts a giant chair with a broken leg and stands across the street from the Palace of Nations in Geneva. The tram stop next to this chair was my regular hopping point to catch tram number 11, which would take me to Gare Cornovain—the city centre. I have always admired the location and facilities this convention centre provides through its multiple halls and grand view, amenities and networking area. I always wondered if something like this could ever be built by us to host scientific events and perhaps even a WHO Global Forum. Back then, that looked like a far-fetched dream, though.

As the announcement of the dates for the fourth WHO Global Forum grew closer, I had put forth a plea to the MoHFW, GoI, to host the forum in India instead of Geneva. My request was conveyed in a most reassuring manner to the WHO with the help of Dr Poonam, who was heading the Health Department of Andhra Pradesh at that time and Ms Preeti Sudan, the then health secretary of the GoI. With the help of charismatic Mr Henk Beckedam, then WHO India office head and Dr Madhur Gupta from the WHO country office, who was also our close colleague and part of the KIHT executive body, it was finally decided that the Global Forum would take place in India. It was probably supposed to be held in some large metro city capable of handling large delegations with a sizable number of hotels; the obvious choice to host the much-acclaimed event would've been New Delhi.

It was already the fourth week of August. I decided to make a second request. As the Global Forum was being hosted in India, could it be at Vizag, at the AMTZ? The immediate response was, 'What? The AMTZ? That's not even fully built?' Once again, Dr Poonam promptly approached the MoHFW in New Delhi with my request to host the forum in Vizag, the city of destiny and in all probability, coincide it with the inauguration of the AMTZ, which was being painstakingly built at breathtaking speed.

During that phase of organizational development and construction, the work was hectic: timelines, construction of complex infrastructure, equipment installations, hiring, business development and, most importantly, building the team of scientists. I would carry two tablets of sublingual nitroglycerine in my purse and keep two of them under my pillow for the few hours I got sleep. I was worried that with thousands of production and testing equipment, the rapid pace of construction that had 2,000 people working in three shifts, financial and technological issues, and the WHO

Global Forum, if there would be any sign of a heart attack. If ever it came to that, I could quickly take the nitroglycerine tablet which is given as the first-response medicine under such conditions.

On 5 September 2018, we received formal communication from the MoHFW that the Fourth WHO Global Forum would be hosted in Vizag from 13 to 15 December 2018. We did not know whether to clap our hands or clasp our jaws. Vizag—yes, great! Where in Vizag would we host it, we did not know. Every Sunday after 5 September, my team and I went around the city looking for all available convention centres. The requirement was unique. The Global Forum needed at least seven halls, one among them for a plenary session; therefore, it needed to be large enough to accommodate over 2,000 people. We also needed six other halls for parallel technical sessions, each with the capacity to accommodate 100–200 people. Besides, the proposed venue would also need a large space for the exhibition of technical dossiers, posters and publications, a large air-conditioned food court and an area for the display of innovations and prototypes of medical devices that would be flown over from across the globe by representatives of over 100 countries numbering over 2,000 professionals, global healthcare leaders and diplomats.

To our surprise—of all the convention centres that we visited in the city—we could find none that matched the requirements. Most convention centres had one large multi-purpose hall, which, although well-equipped, could handle one large gathering at a time and had no other place for parallel or breakout sessions. Convention centres used this hall for hosting weddings, technical seminars and public meetings. It had no room for the translators that would be required in a multilingual conference. Certainly, it did not have a food court capable of hosting about 2,000 people attending any such event, some arrangements being made on a temporary basis as and when required. We were very quickly running out of time. We could only delete the names, one after the other, of convention centres, from the list of available places to host the Global Forum. It was also a matter of great concern as the GoI had already agreed to host the prestigious event. I was also required to share the details, layout drawings, and a list of available facilities at the venue where the Global Forum would be hosted.

At one point in time, on 18 September, after not being able to accept any available convention centre as the desired venue, we decided to build a convention centre to host the Global Forum. It was a crazy idea! A facility was about to be built for an event, although if built at a place like the AMTZ, this convention centre would be of great use for all technical and business events of the Zone in the times to come. But, it was hard to think of building the convention centre, making arrangements for over 2,000 people and continuing to build the AMTZ at a rapid pace so that its inauguration could happen in December along with the Global Forum. The only easy part was that we had less than three months to do all of this.

On 27 September 2018, with the available machinery, materials and as many construction workers as we could mobilize, we laid the foundation of, perhaps, the world's fastest built convention centre. It was a monumental structure that was proposed to have seven conference halls with a total capacity of hosting 2,500 people at any given point of time, consisting of a food arena, a poster presentation area and an innovation display area. The conference halls were required to be equipped with a live transmission set-up and IT equipment and the entire centre needed to be centrally air-conditioned. It would need to have amenities like a coffee shop and networking space. To be honest, we just believed that all this was possible without realizing the enormity of the task.

We progressed with a very stringent construction

plan, a thrice a day construction review and the most disciplined monitoring of work's pace. Millions of pounds of concrete, thousands of tons of steel, hundreds of tons of glass, HVAC equipment capable of providing over 1,000 tons of air-conditioning and the rest of it; ensuring that all these not only arrived in time but were also put in place according to the engineering and architectural designs with precision and at an unimaginable pace was an audacious task. Besides these relatively larger components of the convention centre building, there were also relatively smaller issues. There were matters such as sourcing over 2,500 chairs of the same make, audio and video equipment of good quality, lights and million other atomic components that make up a convention centre. Getting them on time was, in itself, a feat to be admired. And of course, the quality and safety could not be compromised upon. All this would make the Kalam Convention Centre, which was dedicated to the wonderful public life of late Dr A.P.J. Abdul Kalam—the people's president and one of the most beloved scientist technocrat in the Indian modern era. A bust of Dr Kalam crafted in two-dimensional perforated steel, that would make the front facade of the convention centre, was kept as a major design attraction, welcoming and blessing bright minds into what would be a grand knowledge-sharing platform for decades to come. From 27 September to 12 December, there had to be some magic happening continuously to get the convention centre in place for the conference and celebrate the birth of the AMTZ, the world's first medical equipment manufacturing zone. The WHO Global Forum was the most impactful and appropriate event to demonstrate this success.

The operational aspects included food arrangements for 2,000 people for three days, booking every single hotel in the city, all of which put together had just about 2,200 rooms, visa support letters to thousands being sent in coordination with the WHO's team, local police for security, logistical arrangements for the guests from all the hotels to the campus of the AMTZ, fire brigades and ambulance arrangements, travel desk at airports, foreign exchange desks at the convention centre and coordinating with the offices of all dignitaries including ministers, technocrats and officials of the GoI who would grace the occasion. It was a great opportunity for the healthcare technology leaders in India to get exposure to a galaxy of international experts and vice-versa. We also needed to carve out time for our international friends to enjoy Indian culinary skills and experience the culture of the region as many of them were visiting India for the first time.

From Malawi to Massachusetts and Timor Leste to Toronto, we had guests from extremely wide geographic, cultural, ethnic and economic backgrounds. Thanks to Adriana Velazquez, the medical devices unit head at the WHO, Geneva, some delegates from Low and Middle-Income Countries (LMICs) were even sponsored by the WHO to attend the Global Forum. The forum also displayed India's ancient philosophy of *vasudheiva kutumbakam*—'the world is one family'.

Given that a construction schedule would, more often than not, run late, despite the best efforts of engineers and work contractors, I thought of a dry run two days prior to the WHO Global Forum. Accordingly, I spoke to the organizers of a medical conference scheduled to take place in Bengaluru in the first week of December 2018, to be shifted to Vizag on the 10 and 11 December. This would not only give us a dry run but would also push the engineering and construction teams to continue the construction work at full pace before the actual date of inauguration. It seemed very cruel at the time but was a safe and formidable decision. Ten task groups, each led by one of the senior professionals at the AMTZ, took care of the various roles for the WHO Global Forum. From food to facilities, logistics to audio-visuals, we had it covered. Our meeting halls were named just a week before, so placards and signages for the halls were to arrive by 9 December.

Every night, on my way back home, I would study the plans for the next day of work and complete many other smaller tasks like coming up with names of the halls in the convention, streets and avenues at the AMTZ campus. I would name various centres and communicate those names to the engineering team on WhatsApp to get the designs in place. When the signages were put on 10 December—Sigma, Omega, Tesla, Faraday, Curie, Celsius for the six halls and Ampere for the plenary hall, everything looked picture perfect. For the week before the WHO Global Forum and the inaugural date of the AMTZ, the very few hours that I would usually sleep for, were instead, spent in the office, thus ensuring midnight construction site reviews and helping myself start the next day as soon as the morning sun rose.

There was also one little hitch. The AMTZ was being set up in a place that was an unused, thinly spread forest area. The place did not have a ZIP/PIN code yet. Oh! The number of letters and post mails that never reached us or were returned from post offices for want of a ZIP/PIN code has not been documented. We had to apply for a ZIP/PIN code quickly. The AMTZ finally received the code 530031 by the close of October 2018.

In parallel, a high-tension electrical supply line was laid from the nearest power station, which was 23 kilometres away. The line had to travel 14 kilometres overhead, about nine kilometres underground and underneath a railway track for about 500 metres on its way to the AMTZ campus. Similarly, a water pipeline was laid from a reservoir 17 kilometres away, bringing in about 4,500 kilolitres per day (1 kilolitre=1000 litres). It was a mini-city being built with all supportive urban infrastructure and a convention centre to host a global event.

Finally, the day of 13 December 2018 arrived. Thousands of cars and buses brought state and central government guests, speakers, delegates and UN officials into the MedTech city built in just 342 days to participate in a global gathering being hosted in a convention centre that was built in just 78 days. After the AMTZ inaugural plaque was laid under the National Flag, a structure that weighs 17 tons and rises 108 feet tall with the Indian National Flag spanning 10x8 metres, the gathering of dignitaries moved into the Kalam Convention Centre. Apart from the then chief minister of the Andhra Pradesh, there were ministers of Union Government of India, including those from the Ministries of Health and Family Welfare, Commerce, etc., members of the NITI Aayog, which is the highest policy-making body in India, scores of officials in public service representing multiple departments, and hundreds of dignitaries. It was a collective sense of success and progress that prevailed. The three-day conference saw a variety of technical sessions, well-architected by Adriana Velazquez. The Fourth Global Forum created a record of its own. It became the most attended forum till date, with participants from 103 countries. It had a sizable number of technical sessions—as many as 72 sessions! From nomenclature to adverse events reporting, from innovation management to specifications—the technical session witnessed some of the best minds on the subjects from across the globe.

Dr Vinod Paul, a member of the NITI Aayog, mentioned in his remark that if medical devices were to be discussed ever in India, they would always be a 'before-AMTZ' era and an 'after-AMTZ' era. When Ms Subhra Singh, the then chairperson of the National Pharmaceutical Pricing Authority, witnessed the awe-inspiring story of the AMTZ, she exclaimed, 'This is called the audacity of hope'. I could never forget these statements as they represented the collective passion, focus and determination of one of the youngest public sector organizations in the country. It also showcased our ability, anchored by our determination and selflessness, to welcome the world to visit us, celebrate, share and learn. An international event of this scale enhanced the confidence of international delegates in Indian MedTech infrastructure and strengthened India's aspirational positioning as the MedTech destination of the world.

Given that all the directors on the board of the AMTZ travelled and joined the programme, we had our board meeting on the afternoon of 14 December in my office. I thanked the board profusely for their support and, for the first time, despite being in a very professional environment, I had tears rolling down my cheeks. The mission to build the world's first medical technology park with several gigantic structures, scores of factories, installation of thousands of equipment, successfully inviting credible research and manufacturing organizations and bringing the world's most prestigious medical technology event to India and that too to the newly built AMTZ, a task that carried an an astounding weight, was complete with spectacular success. The board was kind enough to pour appreciation and kindest wishes for further progress of the group of organizations that I had just built. A board member even opined that I be nominated for a national award. The very mention of it made me grateful.

During the three-day festival of medical technology,

we also hosted a dinner for thousands of delegates at the beautiful beach hotel, The Park, on 14 December. Sprawling lawns, waves of peace emanating from the sea and multi-cuisine food; everything had been beautifully arranged. Besides, we had our wild card! The brand ambassador of the AMTZ and a perfect 'opener'—Virendra Sehwag, one of the fiercest batsmen that Indian cricket has produced. Sehwag, a joy to all cricket-loving fans, had agreed to be with us for two days. My friend and a global clinical engineering leader, Tom Judd, along with Adriana, welcomed the delegates for the cultural programme and dinner. We had sand art animation chronicle the making of the AMTZ and projected it on a large screen to the thrill of everyone. Geeta, our human resource department head and a prolific dancer, along with her dance group, led a performance of Bharatnatyam, an Indian classical dance form, that caught everyone by surprise. It was a night of fun and joy, peace and celebration.

I had a plate of food in my hand as I watched the guests enjoy the evening. Sitting by my side was my wife Deepti, someone who had silently sacrificed a lot and was witness to my habit of keeping the heart attack-preventing nitroglycerin tablets under my pillow while I caught a few hours of sleep every night. Her steadfastness and commitment to the task I took up, the sincerity with which she supported my duty, the numerous times she turned up at midnight to meet me while I was busy supervising construction, was all too pure and selfless.

Dr Poonam, the chairperson of the board of the AMTZ, whose support gave me tremendous strength to pull off this feat, came to us and asked me if I was happy to see my ambition come to fruition before me. I looked around at the thousands of delegates enjoying their evening after witnessing an astounding WHO Global Conference in the MedTech city built as an example to the rest of the world. I simply said, 'I am satisfied'. I remain truly satisfied with what I could do. Those wishes and congratulatory words still ring in my ears. Even today, when I meet colleagues from Canada or Zambia or Mexico or the UK or any other country in any medical technology meeting around the world, many come up to tell me—'Hey! I visited Vizag to attend the Global Forum at the AMTZ. It was a thrilling experience'.

The concluding day of the conference, 15 December, started with a surprise. The weatherman had given a warning of a cyclone hitting the beach city on the night of 15 December or the forenoon on 16 December. I wondered what would have happened if this prediction had been made for even a day earlier. We were hosting scores of parallel sessions in the conference on various topics of immense importance to healthcare and medical technology. Leading experts from across the world shared the best practices which, if followed, could change the world for the better. Many of those deliberations, like those on medical devices standards and safety protocols, innovation acceleration and focused research, came to the rescue during the COVID-19 pandemic. On the night of 15 December, it started to pour heavily along with the high-velocity winds of a cyclone. By the noon of 16 December, all incoming and outgoing flights were cancelled. But by then, all except two guests had boarded and left for connecting destinations. Our guest counter at the airport, where the AMTZ staff were busy, supported guests round the clock.

The valedictory session of the Fourth WHO Global Forum and the culmination of the inaugural event of the AMTZ was a very touching event. Adriana Velazquez was emotional during her speech and unable to control her tears of joy for helping bring the global MedTech family together. Virendra Sehwag was honest. As a visitor to the AMTZ campus in October, just two months ago, I had shown him the empty ground promising to host him again at the Global Forum at the convention centre after two months, whose foundations did not even exist then. With pride and surprise, he said, 'There was nothing here. Dr Jitendra promised me that there will be a city, a convention centre and a WHO global event. I did not believe it then. Today, as I stand as part of this event and this progress, rest assured we will put a collective effort to help bring affordable medical devices to the country and to the world.' I was privileged to make the concluding vote of thanks. Firstly, I thanked my team whose commitment helped us rise to the occasion; to the WHO, whose assurance gave us confidence; to our colleagues and friends from across the globe who came to be part of this historic and humongous effort; and to all our partners in medical technology who gave us their blessings to build the medical technology capital of India. I invited them to be with us every year to host a similar global medical technology conclave. I promised that we would work with all of them and together we would make medical technology more affordable, accessible and equitable and that we would, through the AMTZ and all its efforts, bring more peace, progress and growth into the world.

8

MADE IN LOCKDOWN

The mystery, the suddenness, the enormity of the novel Coronavirus caught the entire world off guard. It startled us, it numbed us and nobody really knew how to counter or contain it. As the world grappled with this unprecedented pandemic, India, too, was no exception. With our huge population being vulnerable to contagious diseases due to the high population density, it posed a never-before-seen public healthcare challenge to the government and medics.

As the cure is not known, the ensuing battle was all

about saving the lives of infected people and preventing infection in others. As it is a disease that causes acute respiratory problems that result in weak lungs that are unable to supply the required oxygen level to the blood and body, ventilator support becomes critical while dealing with infected patients.

'When the going gets tough, the tough get going'. This epithet perfectly sums up how the AMTZ rose to the COVID-19 challenge and created capabilities and products at lightning speed in service of the country—to protect its huge, vulnerable population from a catastrophe.

In the pre-COVID-19 era, not only India but even the entire world put together had never needed ventilators in such huge quantities. But suddenly in 2020, it became the most essential life-saving mass medical device in medical history. Unfortunately, India had never manufactured ventilators until then as almost all the ventilators available in India were only through imports. And given the high demand and panic in almost every country, it was not something which could be imported quickly and in large quantities. Most countries, by then, had put ventilators and other cardio-respiratory products under the export restriction list.

Many other products were required, some as simple

as medical-grade face masks for the army of medics and care providers. We did not even have the capacity to supply that to the extent it was required or at a speed which was necessary to ensure pan-India availability.

In March 2020, Prof. VijayRaghavan, the principal scientific advisor to the GoI, asked a group of people from different scientific institutions to urgently attend a video call and share their current plans and discuss the strategy of producing scientific medical products quickly. In the meeting, he convinced everyone to change gears very quickly and asked me to draft a proposal to rapidly scale up the manufacturing of ventilators and RT-PCR kits. To be honest, at that point in time, except for Italy, which had seen a sudden rise in the number of cases and mortality due to COVID-19, most other countries had not seen a deathly surge. Prof. VijayRaghavan, a biologist himself, had his hand on the pulse of the emerging situation. With a very affirmative and convincing tone, he made it clear that we all understood the gravity of the rapidly changing situation and prepared to respond in a manner that meets our scientific strengths and the myriad of needs of the COVID-19 context that we were yet to see. The immediate requirements were ventilators, PPE, N95 masks, infrared non-touch thermometer, Bi-PAP, C-PAP, multi-parameter physiologic monitors and most importantly—RT-PCR kits for scale-up of testing. India, at that time, produced zero ventilators, less than 10,000 kits of RT-PCR for tuberculosis, and less than 25,000 PPE kits per day. The requirement was conservatively anticipated to about 50,000 ventilators, one million RT-PCR kits a day and about five million PPE kits and N95 masks a day.

I was returning from Delhi by the 7.25 p.m. flight and the overview that Prof. Vijaya Raghavan gave that afternoon necessitated that I formulate the plan as quickly as possible. I started making a technical proposal on my flight from Delhi to Vizag and named it COMMAND Strategy. 'COMMAND' was an acronym for COVID-19 MedTech Manufacturing and Development. The entire plan was quickly sent to the PSA and subsequently approved and shared with the DBT for further coordination. At the DBT, the secretary, Dr Renu Swaroop, was already working harder than all of us. Her scope included medical technology, vaccine research, access to biological samples and programmatic components of COVID-19 response. With the firm support of Dr Renu and Prof. VijayRaghavan, the COMMAND proposal was, in principle, approved. This included a gigantic scale-up of the production machinery for mass production of ventilators and RT-PCR diagnostic kits in record time, setting up a national supply chain and supporting innovation during the COVID-19 response. There was also a game of providence behind all of this.

On the evening a day before, I was in the office of Dr P.D. Vaghela, the then secretary of the Department of Pharmaceuticals. Dr Vaghela—a very energetic and unassuming administrator, is known to keep himself very accessible to those who are sincere in their professional approach and have sector-specific knowledge resources. During his tenure at this office, I must have visited him over 200 times for various technical discussions and meetings. My phone number was perhaps on his speed dial list for matters relating to medical technology. In one of the passing remarks, he mentioned that the Ministry of Finance was working with the World Bank to enable quick investments to scale up health products manufacturing. For some reason unknown to me, I asked him who was dealing with the matter. He connected me to the joint secretary in the Ministry of Finance almost immediately, and the next day, I was in the office of the joint secretary to seek his advice. At the scheduled time of the meeting, the joint secretary had to rush for another meeting and his office requested that I wait for an hour. Had we had the meeting at the scheduled time, I am not sure the wonderful and providential meeting that happened an hour later would have actually occurred.

As I waited, a group of three gentlemen in suits walked into the office of the joint secretary. I did not know any of them. The three of them were called earlier for another urgent meeting and were the reason I was asked to wait for an hour. As I was invited into the office of the joint secretary, he introduced me to the other two gentlemen. That was the biggest surprise of the day. One gentleman was the head of the World Bank office in India, and the other gentleman was the head of the ADB in India. I could not have asked for more. The ADB head was well aware of the AMTZ, the ADB being the financers of the AMTZ phase two general infrastructure development works. He was very appreciative of the AMTZ project. I explained how investing in production machinery would not only lead to supply of products, but would also support component value chain manufacturing and sustainable livelihood, especially, in a sector like medical technology, which is just coming to prominence.

It took less than five minutes for the people around the table to give my request and the plan the go-ahead. Mr Junaid Ahmed, the country head of the World Bank mentioned that the World Bank had already co-financed projects with the DBT, and this would fit perfectly into the project guidelines. In fact, given the uncertainty around what became an unprecedented global crisis in the next two months, the three angels in that meeting requested that I work at rocket speed to implement the plan that I had proposed. I still vividly remember what Mr Junaid Ahmed said that day. 'This is the kind of thing we are interested in. Let us go ahead at the best speed and be an example to the world!'

I had not imagined that an accidental mention made by Dr P.D. Vaghla the previous evening, and my unplanned meeting with the joint secretary, Ministry of Finance, could result in the providential presence of the heads of two large multinational financing corporations in the same room. It is perhaps one of the biggest fortunate accidents I will always remember. With the World Bank on board, the COMMAND strategy proposal was quickly sent to Dr Renu Swaroop, secretary, DBT, who, by then, had already received the proposal from the office of Prof. VijayRaghavan. Dr Renu Swaroop generally does not miss a moment on any good project and puts the wheel of assessment and action in motion, supporting rapid implementation. With financing for scale-up machinery, a request for proposals was advertised to select industry partners and innovators who would work with us for rapid development, and with the large-scale infrastructure and testing facilities provided at the AMTZ, increase manufacturing by almost 1,000 times. What emerged was, perhaps, one of the largest manufacturing consortiums in record time. Several technological giants, budding entrepreneurs, scientific minds and a pool of facilitators got together. From planning in the fourth week of February to the selection of industry partners by mid-March, and project initiation by the end of March, on the first day of the national lockdown (24 March 2020), the production plan was put in place very rapidly.

Within two weeks of the lockdown, the first RT-PCR kit for COVID-19 was rolled out of the AMTZ campus on 7 April 2020, World Health Day. There couldn't have been a more emphatic expression of commitment, strategy and opportunity to give India high-scale production capability. This was an excellent example of how supportive governance and progressive science could be brought together to address immediate and futuristic priorities.

The COMMAND Strategy had three distinct focal points:

1. Encouraging start-ups and innovators that have taken support from the DBT/BIRAC for

medical technology projects that could support the COVID-19 response. All these innovators and entrepreneurs were to be supported by the AMTZ, technologically facilitated towards the next level of product realization, testing and validation and facilities for prototyping and batch production.

2. Many medical device manufacturers who may have the potential to make critical equipment like ventilators and diagnostic kits, thermal scanners or medical textiles are much needed during the COVID-19 period as well as the post-COVID-19 period. However, to rapidly scale up manufacturing, investment in plants and machinery would be required, without which such a scale-up would not be possible. The DBT-AMTZ COMMAND strategy, therefore, came as a comprehensive solution for a rapid scale-up of infrastructure and production capabilities.

3. Drafting of appropriate standards and safety norms, validation protocols for these medical technologies such as ventilators, N95 masks and so on would be an important area of support to ensure that their quality and safety are upheld. At the same time, we needed to ensure their

registration on the government e-marketplace (GeM). This needed partnership and structure working with institutions such as the BIS, the ICMR and GeM.

On the 7 April, with the ICMR approving the TrueNat test, the RT-PCR kit was launched from an existing licenced facility at the AMTZ. An initial manufacturing capacity of 3,000 RT-PCR COVID-19 kits in April 2020 at one production centre was increased to produce almost a million kits a day by April 2021 across seven production centres. The initial production capacity of 10 ventilators a week became a capacity of about 200 a day, 500 N95 masks a day became 1,00,000 N95 masks a day, and gradually the AMTZ became a source for multiple products such as infrared thermometers, multi-parameter monitors, defibrillators and other essential supplies. Today, close to 200 essential medical technologies including humongous structures such as mobile container-based COVID-19 eight-bedded insolation ICU units and mobile RT-PCR vans.

On the day the national lockdown was announced, the first step was to have the AMTZ campus declared an essential services zone. A notification to this effect was released by the Department of Industries within hours of the lockdown announcement. The entire experience was new. Thousands of factory workers, engineers and the rest of the staff came from various parts of the city, crossing the barricades and road stops with the AMTZ badge and essential services letter displayed on their bikes or cars. Staff residing in areas that would dynamically become 'hot spots' led to the staff commuting by crossing many barriers. The understanding with which the families of the staff have supported them has helped them rise to the occasion. Many people working at the AMTZ lived in self-isolation within their homes, staying away from family members while exposing themselves to the risk of transmission at the factory shop floors and research laboratories. Perhaps the lush green campus of the AMTZ with over 2,00,000 plants and minimal emissions, thanks to the renewable energy solar plant, deserves the true credit of keeping the zone environment clean and healthy for all.

Our day would start at 9.00 a.m., and we usually worked till midnight. A nerve-wracking schedule of work followed. Sourcing of raw materials, components coming from multiple cities and countries had to cross major barriers. Thankfully, customs worked full time and posted additional staff at most customs clearance locations at major ports and airports. Positive cases within the manufacturing lines and product development centres were another difficulty. Yet, between endpoints of the first and the second COVID-19 waves, over 3,000 trucks carried essential medical supplies from the AMTZ to the rest of the country. Due to the fragmented logistics and supply chain, the biggest problem was to get spare parts, critical components and raw materials. Eventually, many of them got indigenized within the zone. Today, the AMTZ makes various critical components such as oligos, primer, probes for in-vitro diagnostic kits, printed circuit boards, and oxygen and flow sensors for medical electronic equipment on its own campus and has its own packaging and sterilization unit for quality packaging.

In the first wave of COVID-19, one team was dedicated to mapping specifications and generating market intelligence for each product segment of the IVDs, ventilators and medical textiles. The second team was supported engineering design, and the third followed up on production machinery, installation and commissioning. The manufacturers also needed to recruit human resources, which was a role performed well by the HR team of the AMTZ led by Geeta Varalakshmi. Recruiting hundreds of technicians and engineers and training them quickly for the production process was a huge task. Logistics and regulatory support teams were also quickly added to work with manufacturing partners. Gradually, we developed a comprehensive network to tame multiple logistical challenges like getting crucial shipments out of containment zones in Pune, Noida, Mumbai, Bangalore, Hyderabad, Delhi, Chandigarh, Coimbatore and Chennai.

Facilitating the logistics of newly recruited human resources was not easy either, as their families pleaded with them to postpone joining at new locations. Selflessness eventually prevailed in most decisions, and the AMTZ could fully provide sufficient human resources to all centres and production facilities. The biggest risk was taken by those that travelled far and wide into the nook and corners of the country to install the equipment that was supplied. Private hospitals, nursing homes from many cities depended daily on supplies from AMTZ.

As a result of these fast-paced initiatives, a momentum was set for greater milestones. Over 100 teams worked across various manufacturing units in two to three shifts a day. Also, showing true team spirit, these manufacturing partners never compared or competed with each other. Rather, we initiated a collaborative working arrangement among these manufacturers as they had their respective R&D or supply chain challenges. Despite the technical difference in their machines/products, they fully extended a helping hand to each other and learned collectively. This collaboration manifested its synergistic effect when the engineering teams of manufacturers, instead of competing, collectively facilitated the process of product development and clinical validations. Satyaki Baneerjee, Maninder Singh, Sashi Kumar, Rajesh Patel, Chandrakeshar Nair, Sriram, Manoj Chugh and Manjiv Singh—leaders from the organizations leading the manufacturing of life saving products—all worked collaboratively to ensure collective success and helped save millions of lives by ensuring rapid supply of critical medical devices.

Just like a whirlpool has unlimited capacity to absorb, the AMTZ, along with its partner companies, absorbed a lot of undue rejection, vested interests, concocted reports, untrue criticism and cynical opinions in the larger interest of the nation as well as patient care. For some reason, one particular reporter had fallen in love with the work of the AMTZ and exhibited that affection by unduly attacking good work, with a friend of the reporter doing the same on twitter. When each positive case was a matter of concern, an attacking article was published by the reporter about the first COVID-19 positive case from the campus, accusing the AMTZ management of being elusive and negligent. On the

India–UK partnership on innovation promotion, another article by the same reporter tried to malign the work, forcing the UK consulate to call off the partnership. The start-ups having been selected already, the AMTZ did not let them down and provided conclusive support by itself. Based on the initial feedback received from hospitals on ventilators, the article declared the AMTZ-made ventilators as substandard. It did not take long for the AMTZ to receive successful test reports required for each product. All such articles were written by a single reporter for a single paper; perhaps the greatest disservice the reporter did to the country was unduly criticizing the life-saving work an organization of the stature of the AMTZ and its partners were doing with utmost dedication.

We received additional support when Mr Ravi Capoor, secretary, Ministry of Textiles, GoI, in March 2020, was called to take the lead in the manufacturing of medical textiles. In just 22 days, a state-of-the-art PPE and mask making centre, TEXTURA, was set up. The decision to manufacture was followed by adequate resource and time allocation for timely deliverables for each product.

In a normal course, product development is a very systematically organized and controlled process that spans a few years. But in the grim situation of the pandemic, we had technical specifications to start and product engineering to advance in less than two or three weeks. We put up a common procurement plan for all manufacturing partners and centralized procurement of critical components to enhance our collective bargaining power. This reduced the delivery time significantly. Wherever necessary, Indian missions aboard were requested to help in sourcing critical components. Indian embassies and consulates based in the US, Japan, China and several countries in Europe provided necessary coordination and support. Dr Arabinda Mitra, scientific secretary in the office of the principal scientific advisor to the GoI was always supportive of such coordination. In particular, Ms Mona Khandhar in the Indian Embassy in Tokyo, Japan, and Mr Dhananjay Tiwari at the Indian Mission in Washington D.C., USA, were a tremendous help.

The second wave of COVID-19 came with its own challenge. In one of the submissions to the Empowered Group for Procurement, I suggested the procurement of oxygen concentrators at least to the extent of 25 per cent of the number of ventilators. Ventilators needed intensive care specialists, where oxygen concentrators scored higher in their ability to support rapid response to patients. However, in the panic that came with the first wave, sufficient priority could not be given to the development or procurement of oxygen concentrators as focus was on ventilators. Then the second wave of COVID-19 struck us hard and fast. Never has the need for oxygen been felt so immensely as was in April–August 2021. The most critical component required to make oxygen concentrators—the lithium sieve, also called zeolite, is not made in India yet. France, US, Japan and China remained the major sources and, suddenly, there was a global scarcity of this sieve. Additionally, oil-free compressors were required. Despite our best efforts, the AMTZ could supply only a few thousand oxygen concentrators for the first 30 days. Very quickly again, large-scale indigenization was done for most components and, gradually, oil-free compressors, oxygen sensors and other critical components became part of the AMTZ action plan for indigenization. The AMTZ remains a large supplier to public sector organizations, state governments, the Indian Navy and the Infosys Foundation, and was responsible for saving thousands of lives by ensuring a timely supply of oxygen concentrators. Initially, when the out cabinet of these machines required a standard mould which could have taken six to eight weeks to develop, it was Hindware that came to our rescue. Vikas Manchanda from Hindware ensured that we were supplied with the outer casing of Hindware Air Coolers, which was a perfect match as an enclosure to the various components of the oxygen concentrator. Zeolite production remains an area of work that is to be improved upon. All through the crises, officials such as Sri Ajay Sahani, Sri Sanjay Chadda, Sri Ravi Capoor, Dr P.D. Vaghela, late Sri Guru Mahapatra, whom we lost to COVID-19, Dr Renu Swaroop, Dr Balram Bhargava, Ms S. Aparna, Dr Arabinda Mitra with overarching support from Prof. VijayRaghavan, Dr Vinod Paul and Sri Amitabh Kant at the NITI Aayog, kept the national convergence of capabilities strong enough for the country to tide over the crisis.

Given the long-term effects of COVID-19, I still feel there are areas of product development where urgent attention needs to be given. The AMTZ has started development work on a dialysis machine, extracorporeal membrane oxygenation (ECMO) and cardiac ultrasound and more scientific organizations need to work rapidly to develop these devices, to rule out scarcity in the event of another health disaster. International Health Regulations (IHR) is a principle agreement that WHO supports and recommends compliance across member countries. IHR provides a framework for preparedness, monitoring and implementation of the best practices during disease outbreaks. I feel singularly lucky to have IHR as the thesis title of my doctoral work from years ago. Further, in 2010, along with Dr Shakti Gupta—the then head of the department of hospital administration, AIIMS, New Delhi—I was privileged to co-author the first book on this crucial subject. *Disease Outbreak Management: Hospital Administrators' Perspective,* published by Jaypee Publications, which remains a key practical resource that could further help planning in health facilities, now augmented by the possibility of using technologies to provide better healthcare than ever before.

Medical equipment 'made in lockdown' was the eureka moment of the Indian MedTech sector. It has, for posterity, instilled progress and, most importantly confidence, in the enterprising attitude of those who see their passion and commitment to research and the production of medical equipment. The AMTZ, an established medical technology manufacturing ecosystem, had all that it would need to make it happen and rose to the occasion. The common scientific facilities and common manufacturing facilities, including specialized laboratories, warehousing and testing centres that already existed on campus, were an added advantage for the mission to which the AMTZ was committed. Common scientific and industrial laboratories/centres such as the

Centre for Electromagnetic Compatibility and safety testing, Centre for Biomaterial Testing, Centre for 3D printing, Centre for Lasers, Gamma Irradiation, Moulding and many other industrial service centres, worked together with researchers, entrepreneurs and manufacturers.

As rapid product development found its roots, more systemic designs and large infrastructural facilities became a necessity and also a possibility. The mobile diagnostic unit, infectious disease diagnostic lab (I-Lab), with a biosafety facility capable of RT-PCR, enzyme-linked immunoassay (ELISA) and 30 more tests, was introduced to ensure ease of testing in rural areas. The first I-Lab was inaugurated on 18 June 2020 in New Delhi by the Union health minister. Dr Renu Swaroop—known to give complex tasks to the institutions she trusts—had asked for the mobile testing facility and the first mobile laboratory to be built at the AMTZ in record time of eight days. As of now, several states, particularly in the difficult terrain of Northeast India, deploy these mobile testing laboratories—a wonderful asset for resource constrained settings.

Similarly, container hospitals were built with an entire hospital setting environment with eight beds, oxygen pipeline, supply lines and life-saving equipment fitted into 40x8 feet containers that could be transported by trucks to any place and could be used for providing health services, very much like a hospital, to places which do not have an established clinical setting. Container hospitals that proved to be immensely useful were built at the AMTZ under the name Safe Zone and shipped to over 50 destinations. The request for the mobile container hospitals—safe zones—had come from Prof. VijayRaghavan's office. Oxy-Wheel is a pressure swing adsorption plant for oxygen generation that can cover the oxygen requirement of many hospitals in a single day at a very nominal cost, saving the capital investment required to set up these plants permanently.

Beyond the myriad of products produced at the AMTZ every day, for a country that imports over ₹40,000 crore (approximately $5 billion) of medical equipment every year,[15] the AMTZ aims to produce over ₹20,000 crore ($2 billion) worth of medical equipment per annum. That's almost 50 per cent of India's import dependency.

Medical technology has become a sector that has survived the uncertainties of economic turbulence as

---

[15]'GLOBEXIM 2020–21', Kalam Institute of Health Technology, 2020.

well as showcased its life-saving capacity for social good. Today, the AMTZ stands tall by virtue of its service to the country in protecting the health of the people by supplying affordable, accessible and good-quality products across multiple states and hospitals across all geographical regions. We remain committed to delivering the nation from import dependency and making India a proud leader in medical technology development and production. RT-PCR kits, oxygen concentrators and other products made at the AMTZ are now exported to several countries.

Digital services integrated with medical technology also have immense potential to democratize the adoption of medical technology. We set up a department for digital services (Digi-Serve) which works in brilliant and innovative ways thanks to the huge amount of encouragement we receive from Mr Amitabh Kant, the immensely respected doyen of India's economic growth story, serving as CEO, NITI Aayog, India's premier policy-making body and a national think tank. When a product is expensive and the need for that product is occasional, as is the case with most medical devices, that's when the product becomes a 'service'. This directly impacts penetration, access and affordability. A very simple and life-saving example is the Affordable Oxygen

Concentrator Rental Programme that changed the way families spend money on something as critical as oxygen.

The O2Home, a service designed by the AMTZ's digital service team, is an Affordable Oxygen Concentrator Rental Programme. Built on Android and iOS platforms, it is an application-based service that allows people across 40 major cities in India to book an oxygen concentrator for rent for less than ₹400 than purchase it for ₹60,000. Interestingly, the AMTZ signed a MoU with Uber, India, that allows designated Uber drivers to pick up the booked concentrators from multi-city storage locations and deliver them to the home addresses of those who book the device. The concentrators are collected five to 10 days after the rental subscription is completed. Buying concentrators is still not an option for many households. But renting a concentrator sourced from reliable and safe sources, at a fraction of the cost with doorstep delivery and without any monetary deposit, is exactly what democratizing technology means. Through O2Home, the AMTZ provides access to oxygen for COVID-19 patients as well as people with special medical needs directly to their homes. This not only reduces the pressure on healthcare infrastructure, which is already under stress, but also creates a positive economic value chain by ensuring market access for manufactured products without causing economic hardships to the patients. Many similar services for vision care (V2 Home) and dental care (D2 Home) are now under progressive stages of development at the AMTZ.

Another digital service that serves as an example to innovators is TechOla. Innovators and enterprises need timely, accurate and credible services for product development. Given the lack of knowledge on the availability of these services, we built a marketplace for laboratories and service providers to facilitate an innovator's journey.

TechOla is an integrated digital ecosystem that provides an e-marketplace service connecting the innovators, scientific service providers, researchers and laboratory infrastructure across the country. Its core values are to provide product cushioning to the growing sector of medical devices innovation and manufacturing and speed up prototyping and go-to-market strategy. Innovators can now check, compare, select and pay for the services of any laboratory across India, services they need for product prototyping, testing and validation of batch production. TechOla, available on Android and iOS platforms, also provides consultation and incubation services. There are no membership fees for laboratories or innovators. The entire system is seamless, including logistics for product sample shipments.

TechRx is yet another digital service platform addressing the manufacturers' need for components and spares in medical device manufacturing. The application connects medical equipment manufacturers with electronics spares, components and machinery suppliers. The platform facilitates interaction, exchange of part numbers and pictures of critical parts, spares and components across buyers, sellers and distributors to speed up the searching and buying process. It also helps in finding a comprehensive logistics partner for all shipment needs.

While O2Home is for patients and families that need oxygen therapy at home, TechOla is for innovators and TechRx is for manufacturers. Digital services, therefore, can impact the entire value chain, from patients to manufacturers. The Digi-Serve unit at the AMTZ is expanding rapidly and is on track to launch a number of initiatives. Digi-Serve aims to democratize medical technology, bring in accessibility where possible and, most importantly, affordability for patients who need the support of medical devices.

When all the urgency of the pandemic is behind us, when India is self-reliant in its medical technology needs and when Indian-made medical equipment contributes to global healthcare supplies in a much larger way, perhaps then, the role of the AMTZ would be fully evident. The path-breaking work of converging product development scientists, clinicians, entrepreneurs and manufacturers, all under one umbrella, done in record time under tiring circumstances, is a positively far-reaching task. Setting the discourse of medical equipment sectoral development through institutions like KIHT, the IBSC, among many others, and serving in dire situations in the most formidable manner is the perfect gift of dedication to nation-builders like Dr A.P.J. Abdul Kalam. And then one day, those prophetic remarks of Dr Vinod Paul made during the inauguration of the AMTZ in December 2018 would sound so true—'Whenever the history of growth of medical technology sector in India be written, it will be always mentioned "before the AMTZ" and "after the AMTZ."'

ACKNOWLEDGEMENTS

The acknowledgements for this work are shared in two parts. The first part is for those who helped me create the AMTZ—the ultra-modern facility slated to make India a global hub for medical equipment manufacturing. The second part is for those that helped me document this wonderful journey in the form of this book.

For the first part, my utmost gratitude is to my Guru—Bhagawan Sri Satya Sai Baba, who, by being an example, showed that providing selfless service is the best form of worship. I am grateful to my family, particularly my wife, Deepti, and our parents, who have all remained piously supportive of my efforts. My teachers—Dr Shakti

Gupta, late Dr A.N. Safaya and the late Dr M.R. Patel are pillars of inspiration. Building the AMTZ as a role model in record time was possible only with the support of Smt. Poonam, a civil servant of high probity, and I am thankful to her. Global champions in MedTech and innovation—Tom Judd, David Yadin, Adriana Velazquez, Dr Soumya Swaminathan, Brad Schoener and Louise Agarsnap, deserve my sincere thanks. Stalwarts including Prof. VijayRaghavan, Sri Amitabh Kant, Dr Renu Swaroop, Dr Arabinda Mitra, Sri Rajiv Agarwal, Sri Sanjay Chadda, Sri Ravi Capoor, Dr P.D. Vaghela, Sri Ajay Sahani, Dr Balram Bhargava, Ms S. Aparna, Dr Manish Diwan, Sri Chantan Vishnav, Dr R.K. Srivastava, Dr G.N. Singh and Dr Alka Sharma are gratefully acknowledged for their support. And my deepest appreciation is to my team of scientists and colleagues at the AMTZ—the best family one can have. They are sincere and dedicated to the mission of making India a global leader in medical technology. Rakesh Bhatia, Manish Kishore, Geeta, Dr Kavita, Vivekanand, Shishir, Khasim, Mrutunjaya Jena, Dr Anand, Dilip Kumar, Santosh Balivada, Junaid, Raju, Dr Susheela, Sushmita, Krishnakant, Ravi Vittal, Shahrukh, Prashant, Pavan and hundreds of other colleagues who tirelessly work every day to build better medical equipment for India and the world, all deserve sincere appreciation. Industry colleagues including Rajiv Nath, Suresh Vazirani, Mala Vaziani, Himanshu Baid, Pawan Chaudhary, Vaibhav Garg, Ashoke, Madan Krishnan, Sudhakar, Elizabeth, Shobha, Shravan, Maninder Singh, Manjiv Singh, Mahesh Kapri, Dr G.S.K. Velu, Satyaki, Rajesh Patel, Chandrasekhar Nair and Veena Kohli are all enterprising professionals committed to national growth.

For the second part, I cannot thank enough the efforts made by Shelley Vishwajeet to help this book achieve its final shape. He was frank and extremely supportive of the entire effort and a friend I could rely upon from the moment the idea for this book was conceived. My sincere thanks are also to Manish Rastogi for supporting the fact-finding, collating, and helping me in the initial stages of writing this book. I owe sincere thanks to my colleague Shishir Prabhakar, Vinod and Surya for always being there to help with photographs and designs. I thank Rupa Publications for helping this manuscript reach fruition. Indeed, the story of the AMTZ, which was built in record time, could have only been written and published in record time. A big share of that effort and success is to Ms Yamini Chowdhury, senior commissioning editor, for being wonderfully supportive. I wish to sincerely thank Ms Soumya Rampal for her support in the review and copy-editing of the manuscript, without which, it would have been less than perfect.

I also thank each and every patient who has given us an opportunity to serve their medical needs. It is to them that our lives are dedicated, and we are privileged to serve them.

INDEX